POWERHOUSE writing

High School

Lisa Dettinger

POWERHOUSE
educational resources

© 2019 PowerHouse Educational Resources
Vertical Press Books

ISBN-13: 978-1-7336998-1-5

Cover Design by Kaylee Winsand
Logo by Urban Root Creative
Technical Assistant Heidi Thorstad

*Student essay topics, samples, and sources cited are not representative of the beliefs of this author.

U.S. Copyright Office. All rights reserved. No part of this book may be reproduced in any form without written permission from the publisher. Permission is granted to photocopy templates and work pages for one family or one classroom use only.

Printed in the United States of America.

Table of Contents

	Page
How to Use This Curriculum	3
Lesson 1: Foundations	5
Part A	6
Three Essential Components	
Tools for Improving Sentence Structure	
Part B	10
Transitions	
Three Simple Steps	
MLA Formatting: the Basics	
Lesson 2: Process Essays	15
Part A	17
Citing Within the Text	
Condensing Information	
Part B	22
From Graphic Organizer to Essay	
Writing Body Paragraphs for the Process Essay	
Lesson 3: Cause-Effect Essays	29
Part A	31
Introductions	
Conclusions	
Part B	36
Writing the Cause-Effect Essay	
Lesson 4: Compare-Contrast Essays	43
Part A	45
Block vs. Point-by-Point	
Part B	50
Writing the Compare-Contrast Essay	

Lesson 5: Editorial Essays....55
Part A....57
Diamond Conclusion
Editorial Exercise
Part B....67
Writing the Editorial Essay

Lesson 6: Problem-Solution Essays....73
Writing the Problem-Solution Essay

Lesson 7: Argumentative Essays....85
Part A....87
Organization Options
Affirmative or Negative Exercise
Intro to a Values Debate
Part B....94
Affirmative and Negative Arguments & Evidence
Writing the Argumentative Essay

Lesson 8: Test Preparation....107
Part A....109
Review & Test Preparation
Practicing the Timed Test Using the Tools
Part B....117
Test (printable from website or your USB storage device)

Answer Keys....119

How to Use This Curriculum

1. Log in to PowerHouseEdu.com. Here you can gain access to the online videos or purchase the USB drive for this video course. (The workbook and videos are used concurrently.)

2. Watch the first video segment and interact with this workbook according to the video.

3. Repeat until videos, workbook, and essay assignments are complete.

4. Yes, it's that simple. (You don't need a teacher's guide.)

Notes

- There's an answer key in the back of the workbook. To grade essays, use the rubric included in each lesson. Both the student and the teacher evaluate the essay and rank each line item on the rubric either a 1 (missed it completely), 2 (minimal evidence of this), 3 (good effort and can still improve), or 4 (excellent). Including vocab words warrants extra credit (see rubric). Teachers can opt to write comments about their rankings to provide more feedback for the student as well.

- There are eight titled lessons. Most of them have a "Part A" and a "Part B." There are 15 total video sessions. Most lessons begin with a quiz.

- This course can be completed in a quarter, a trimester, a semester, or a year. You can decide how many days per week to spend on writing and how quickly or slowly you want to move through the course.

- It's worth .5 credit. If you need a full credit of composition for your transcript, simply go back through and write six more essays using different topics. (Also, if you used Graphic Organizer A the first time, use B the second time.)

- Got burning questions? Go to PowerHouseEdu.com.

Lesson 1
Foundations

Lesson 1: Foundations

Three essential components to an excellent essay:

1) _____
   a) 5-P essays
      i) Introduction paragraph (contains thesis)
      ii) Three body paragraphs
      iii) Conclusion paragraph
      iv) Every essay = start and end with thesis, body = main supporting points.
   b) Use graphic organizers
      i) The "meat and potatoes" of organizing essays: simple and visual!
      ii) No need for the long, tedious "writing process"
      iii) Memorize the shapes and you can instantly visualize the organization of any essay.
   c) Repeat process
      i) One semester-long essay project vs. several 5-paragraph essays
      ii) Adept at the 5-paragraph essay = adept at any academic writing

2) _____
   a) Not redundant
   b) Valuable info broken into bite-sized pieces
   c) Well-supported points

   i) I love going to California because the scenery is beautiful. I like to look at the mountains and the beach because they are so pretty. When I see the landscape of California, I realize how gorgeous it is.

   ii) Topanga Canyon Boulevard in southern California is one of my favorite places. The arid climate, ample sun, bright cactus flowers, and unique structures along the drive make for a very pleasant journey. After a few miles of a windy ascent, we are compelled to pull over so we can ogle at the San Fernando Valley until the lure of the ocean finally motivates us to peel our eyes from the view. When we crest the mountainous terrain, the spectacular view of the Pacific takes my breath away and I am rendered speechless. As we carefully maneuver our way downward, we roll down the windows and inhale the salty freshness of the approaching beach. The journey through

Topanga Canyon is an overview of all the best California has to offer, which is why I rank it so highly.

3) _____
   a) Command of complex structure of English
   b) Long, complex sentences punctuated with a short one

      i) *These statistics are disturbing. Youth who spend more than 10 hours a week playing video games are in trouble. "Grand Theft Auto" is one example. High school students in Detroit, Michigan did something about it. They developed a cogent and inspiring presentation at their high school. This led to an all-school boycott for video games not rated "E" for everyone. This was a very impressive feat!*

      ii) *Statistics such as these reveal disturbing consequences for youth who spend more than ten hours per week absorbed in violent, anti-moral video games such as "Grand Theft Auto." Recently, a group of concerned high schoolers in Detroit, MI developed a cogent and inspiring presentation for their public school peers which led to an all-school boycott of any video games not rated "E" for everyone. This was no small feat.*

   c) Strong verbs
      i) ~~Walking~~/striding, ~~tell~~/promulgate, ~~left~~/exited
   d) Vocabulary: use of _____
      i) Infer a solid education of the user.
      ii) Likely to appear on college entrance exams.

Vocabulary for Lesson 1

1. Ubiquitous:

2. Ineffable:

3. Malevolent:

4. Promulgate:

Tools for Providing More Complex Sentence Structure

Read how we can take a basic sentence and improve it by adding some simple variations.

Basic Sentence Structure
Every sentence needs a main subject and a main verb (subject and predicate).

Joe watched the baseball game.
    Subject = Joe
    Verb = watched
    Predicate = watched the baseball game (has the subject's verb in it)

Adding More Powerful Parts of Speech…
Add interest and more specific information with parts of speech such as an adverb and a prepositional phrase.

Throughout the Dodgers game, Joe gazed despairingly at the scoreboard.
    Subject = Joe
    Verb - gazed
    Adverb = despairingly
    Prepositional phrases = throughout the game, at the scoreboard

Throw in an Appositive
Appositives redefine a noun to provide more information.

Throughout the Dodgers game, Joe, a die-hard fan, gazed despairingly at the scoreboard.
    Appositive = a die-hard fan

Play with Syntax
Simply changing the order of your phrases or words can make the sentence more interesting or help it to flow better.

Joe, a die-hard fan, gazed despairingly at the scoreboard throughout the Dodgers game.
    Prepositional phrase moved to the end = throughout the Dodgers game

Add a Clause
Clauses are phrases that can be added to the subject or predicate of a sentence.   Examples include: because, which, though, although, who, or that.

Though he hated to look, Joe, a die-hard fan, gazed despairingly at the scoreboard throughout the Dodgers game.
    Clause = though he hated to look

Try a Gerund
A gerund looks like a verb because of its "ing" ending, but it functions as a noun.

Watching his favorite team was usually enjoyable, but today was a different story. Joe, a die-hard fan, gazed despairingly at the scoreboard throughout the Dodgers game.
    Gerund = watching
    Gerund phrase – watching his favorite team

Putting It All Together
Original sentence: *Joe watched the baseball game.*

Descriptive Paragraph
Watching his favorite team was usually enjoyable, but today was a different story. Joe, a die-hard fan, gazed despairingly at the scoreboard throughout the Dodgers game, his countenance mirroring that of the other fans as each inning brought nothing but

disappointment. Suddenly, a piercing crack abruptly awakened the unsuspecting crowd. A grand slam! Joe, who sat slumped in his seat, leaped to his feet and body-slammed his brother, knocking over their precious bag of peanuts.

Create a short paragraph from the sentence below by incorporating more complex sentence structure. Add a very short, simple sentence for added emphasis.

Sentence: He walked across the bridge.

Improved: _____

Transitions

Whether stated or implied, transitions provide a signal to the reader when a new point is going to be made. They help guide the reader through the essay. Examples of transition words include: first, next, another, also, finally, and in conclusion. Read the following paragraph and note the transitions (in bold type).

*A **third** architectural landmark with a contentious history is the glass pyramid that greets visitors in the courtyard of the Louvre Museum. The debate surrounding this Parisian icon continues today. **For example**, some proponents of the pyramid claim that it symbolizes Paris as an entirely modern city while eliciting a sense of pride in the city's* *rich history.* ***However,*** *opponents to the pyramid insist that the museum grounds should maintain the historic authenticity of the Louvre Palace before it became a world-famous museum. They feel the modernity of Paris is irrelevant when one visits a museum of such historical magnitude.* ***Another*** *debate about the Louvre's pyramid focuses merely on its aesthetic qualities.* ***For example,*** *some French countrymen loathe the appearance of the pyramid, saying that it blocks the beauty of the palace surrounding it.* ***On the other hand,*** *proponents of the pyramid regard it as a symbol of the museum's purpose of invoking a deep appreciation for manifold forms of art.* ***In short,*** *the Louvre Museum's pyramid includes a history of debate for the French, one which will not likely be resolved soon.*

More about transitions:
1. When using the word "first" as a transition, use "second" and "third" as well ("the first reason..." "the second reason..." "the third reason...").
2. Transition words can sometimes be implied rather than stated.
    When Neal Armstrong landed on the moon, he declared it was a "small step for man, but a giant leap for mankind." There are three factors that led to U.S. winning the "space race." J.F. Kennedy catapulted America's involvement in 1961 when he announced that Americans would be in space and on the moon by the end of that decade (space.com staff)...

Two Basic Types of Essays

1. _____: meant to inform, holds an objective view.

2. _____: informs *and* persuades the reader to think or to act.

Writing an Essay in Three Simple Steps

1. Decide which _____ _____ you'll use.

2. Jot down a few words on each line.
    a. Do NOT use _____ _____!

3. Type it *while* incorporating your specific _____.

MLA Formatting

MLA stands for "Modern Language Association" and is a system for documenting sources in scholarly writing. It has been used throughout the world for over 50 years. This standardization for essays emphasizes authorship and is widely used by scholars, journal publishers, and academic and commercial presses (MLA.org).

There are other formatting systems such as APA ("American Psychological Association") and Chicago Manual of Style. APA emphasizes *when* a piece of evidence was documented and is commonly used in the social sciences. CMOS incorporates two systems: a notes and bibliography system and an author-date system. It is commonly used in the fields of science and humanities (owl.purdue.edu).

MLA was updated in 2016. The *MLA Handbook*, the authoritative resource for formatting, is currently in its eighth edition. The MLA typically releases a new edition every ten years. For up-to-date formatting information, you can purchase the latest edition of *MLA Handbook* or go to www.owl.purdue.edu.

Practice using MLA by typing the following two pages.

Lastname 1

Firstname Lastname

Teacher's Name

Class Name

10 April 2019

MLA Basics

Indent each new paragraph. Use ONLY double-spacing throughout your document. Create a header in the far upper right corner of your page that includes your last name and an automated page number. This header will appear on each of your essay's pages. Use italics when typing the name of a book. When citing a source, type a parenthesis, then a period. According to Dettinger, author of *Home Run Essays,* one should always "cite appropriately within the text" (45). If there are references to more than one author in a paragraph, type the author's last name followed by the page number (all in parentheses). Do not use a comma (Grover 26).

> When quoting four lines or more, indent the left margin one inch by dragging your ruler's arrows to the right. At the end of the quote, type the period and put the page number in parentheses. Do NOT use italics or quotation marks for these longer quotes unless there is dialogue within the passage. (15)

Include a Works Cited page as the last page of your essay. There are samples of Works Cited pages in this workbook. Create hanging indents for your entries. Here is an example of a hanging indent from a Works Cited page:

Lewis, C.S. *The Chronicles of Narnia: The Lion, the Witch, and the Wardrobe.* New York: Harper Collins Publishers. 1950. Print.

If you use a website that does not give the author's name, the title of the website article is listed first. This title would be put in the parentheses when cited within the essay also. For example, "Here is a website quote" ("MLA Formatting"). When your essay readers want to refer to any sources you've cited, they will easily find the author's last name or the website article's name because the entries are alphabetized in addition to the hanging indents.

Lesson 2
Process Essays

Quiz #1

Matching

1. _____malevolent   A. (seemingly) everywhere
2. _____ineffable   B. wishing harm to others
3. _____ubiquitous   C. to proclaim or make known
4. _____promulgate   D. not able to express through words

Short answer

5. What are the three essential components to an excellent essay?

_____ _____ _____

6. What are three tools you can use to provide more complex sentence structure?

_____ _____ _____

7. What's the difference between an expository and a persuasive essay?

_____

_____

True or False

8. _____ You should use complete sentences for graphic organizers and outlines.

9. _____ "The first reason," "Another example," and "In conclusion" are examples of transition words that help guide the reader.

10. _____ When using MLA, your Works Cited page should include an alphabetized listing of your sources.

11. _____ MLA is the only formatting method used in universities.

12. _____ Book titles are put in quotation marks for MLA formatting.

Lesson 2: The Process Essay

Vocabulary for Lesson 2

1. Cacophony:

2. Cogent:

3. Veracity:

4. Quagmire:

The **process essay** informs about something that happens in phases, such as the water cycle, insect development, or the stages of mitosis.

To write a process essay:

1) Decide the _____.

2) (Look at the graphic _____.)

3) Simplify your essay's information into _____ _____ _____.

4) Jot a few words in each section of the organizer.

    a) Do NOT write in complete sentences!

    b) Use simple wording to jog your memory.

* Your graphic organizer provides lines for the three main stages, details about those stages, and evidence/data to support the details.

Citing Within the Text

Always *cite* any specific data you present in an essay. These citations will correspond with your Works Cited page. When you cite a source, you are proving your credibility to the reader, giving credit to your source (avoiding plagiarism), and allowing your reader to follow up with his own research.

Examples of sentence structure for citing information in your essay:

1. According to Joe Shmoe, author of *Poultry People*, chickens have barbed feathers (10).

2. Elmer Fudd never did catch that "Wascally Wabbit," but his four million viewers enjoyed watching him try (Stanley).

3. As Gimli so eloquently put it, "Keep breathing. That's the key" (Tolkien).

To practice writing a process essay, we'll use the topic "Starting a Home-based Business as a Teen."

Now we know our thesis.

Next, look at the graphic organizer for the process essay. We know we'll include three basic steps. Each step will have a detail and each detail will have evidence.

To provide evidence for each step, let's create a sample business: dog-walking.

The following page includes an article titled "Starting a Home-based Business as a Teen" by Amanda Brookins. Notice there are eight steps. Read the article and determine which steps are necessary for starting a dog-walking business.

Cross off the numbers that are irrelevant and circle the numbers that give specific, applicable direction to starting a dog-walking business. Underline or highlight the most important information.

Starting a Home-based Business as a Teen

Teen entrepreneurs may choose to start home-based businesses as they recognize the benefits, opportunities and resources available for business owners. Home-based businesses give teens the chance to build a company from the ground up, while working in the comfort and privacy of their own homes. As a teen, you may run your business part time, after school or during summer and winter breaks, so consider your availability as you plan your enterprise. Forming a home-based business may seem like a challenging feat, but with proper planning and preparation, you can run a successful and profitable company.

Instructions

1. Think about your hobbies interests and skills as you come up with ideas on the type of business that you would like to start. Select an idea that you'll have fun doing and that also will be profitable.
2. Discuss the idea of your running your own home-based business with your parents. It's important to include them in your plan from the start, so that they can help you work through areas of concern.
3. Contact your local Chamber of Commerce to find out the rules and regulations for registering a home-based business as a teen. Determine if there are licenses and permits that you need to run the business that you have in mind.
4. Create a mini business plan which outlines your product or service, how you plan to run operations, your financing and marketing strategies. Include a list of the products or services that you plan to offer, along with your pricing and payment terms.
5. Create a schedule for yourself which outlines your school responsibilities, any after school programs and activities that you participate in, your home obligations, such as chores, and your new business schedule. You may opt to work on your business after school or only during the weekends.
6. Find an area of your home that you can use to set up your home-based business. If you have a desk in your room or study already, talk to your parents about using that space as your office. Purchase the supplies and equipment that you need to run your business.
7. Promote your home-based business using marketing tools, such as business cards, brochures, a website, social networks and word-of-mouth. Ask a friend who is skilled in graphic design to help you create the marketing materials that you need to advertise your business. Hang flyers in local stores, on bulletin boards and at community and business centers in your area.
8. Save receipts for all of the money that you spend (expenses) and receive (income). When it's time to file taxes, you'll need that information to complete your forms. As a teen, your parents may include you on their tax return, so they should work with a certified public accountant when it's time to file taxes.

Brookins, Amanda. "Starting a Home-based Business as a Teen." ehow Money. 2012. Demand Media. July 10, 2012. Web.

Process Essay

Intro

Thesis

1st Stage: _____

Support:

* _____ Evidence: _____
* _____ Evidence: _____
* _____ Evidence: _____

2nd Stage: _____

Support:

* _____ Evidence: _____
* _____ Evidence: _____
* _____ Evidence: _____

3rd Stage: _____

Support:

* _____ Evidence: _____
* _____ Evidence: _____
* _____ Evidence: _____

Thesis

Conclusion

©Powerhouse Educational Resources

Next steps:

1) Label the three main stages on your graphic organizer's "stages" lines.
   a) First stage: **Business plan**
   b) Second stage: **Purchase supplies/equipment**
   c) Third stage: **Promote**

2) Write the examples of each stage on the left lines in that shape (support).
   a) Business plan
      i) **Outline products/services**
      ii) **How to run operations**
      iii) **Financing and marketing strategies**

   b) Purchase supplies/equipment
      i) **Determine needs: space & supplies**
      ii) **Purchase**
      iii) **Save all receipts**

   c) Promote
      i) **Marketing materials**
      ii) **Internet**
      iii) **Word-of-mouth**

3) Jot a detail (evidence) about each example using dog-walking. (Use proper nouns for the most specific evidence.)
   a) Business plan
      i) Outline products/services: **just walking or feeding/dog-sitting too?**
      ii) How to run operations: **online vs. phone appointments**
      iii) Financing and marketing strategies: **paid before or after walking?**

   b) Purchase supplies/equipment
      i) Determine needs: space & supplies: **desk/office? Leashes? Treats?**
      ii) Purchase: **Animart, Petsmart, Walmart; sales**
      iii) Save all receipts: **keep records + tax purposes**

   c) Promote
      i) Marketing materials: **flyers, cards, "Happy Canines Walking"**
      ii) Internet: **social media (Facebook), website, emails**
      iii) Word-of-mouth: **tell Aunt Sally, neighbor Bob, & friends to spread the word**

Notice the triangle shapes for the introduction and conclusion. You will practice introductions and conclusions in the next lesson. In essence, the wide part of the introduction triangle symbolizes getting the reader's attention (AKA "the hook"). The point at the bottom symbolizes the thesis. For the conclusion, you'll start with the thesis (the "point" of your essay) and end with a statement that leaves the reader thinking.

From Graphic Organizer to Essay

Now it's time to practice writing three body paragraphs using the graphic organizer as your guide. The introduction and conclusion paragraphs are written for you on page 23. Your job is to:

1. Write a sentence that includes your words on the "stage" line. Be sure to use transition words. (*The **first step** in starting a home-based business as a teen is to create a **business plan**.*)

2. Your next sentence will include the words from your first example in that shape. (*Your business plan will include an **outline** of your **products and services**.*)

3. The next sentence in this first stage will be your evidence/data to support that sentence. (*For example, will you be merely walking the dogs or will you also offer to **feed or dog-sit** for pets?*)

4. Continue creating sentences from each line-item in your graphic organizer. Be sure to indent each new paragraph.

*Note: The beauty of this system is its simplicity. Typically, you'll fill out a graphic organizer *while* brainstorming and immediately type your essay in complete sentences *while* incorporating your evidence.

Starting a Home-based Business as a Teen

If you're a typical teen, you're looking for ways to earn some extra cash. Starting a home-based business may seem like a daunting task, but if you recognize a need in your community for a particular product or service (such as dog-walking), owning your own business can be very rewarding. With proper planning and preparation, you'll be on your way to a successful home-based business, which will be a win-win for you *and* Fido!

_____

Any teen can start a home-based business to earn some extra cash. All it takes is a solid business plan, the right equipment, and good marketing to get it off the ground. With these key factors in place, you're sure to succeed. Fido's tail will wag profusely during his daily walk, and you'll have extra cash in your pocket. So what are you waiting for?

Process Essay Rubric

	Student	Teacher
Ideas		
Clearly defined thesis	_____	_____
Supportive details in body	_____	_____
Depth of Knowledge	_____	_____
Holds reader's attention	_____	_____
Organization		
Paragraphs		
Intro (attention-getter, tie-in, thesis)	_____	_____
Body (in chronological order)	_____	_____
Conclusion (summary of thesis, tie-in, closure)	_____	_____
Appropriate transitions	_____	_____
Voice		
Demonstrates writer's interest in topic	_____	_____
Uses creative expressions, images	_____	_____
Word Choice		
Powerful verbs	_____	_____
Specific nouns	_____	_____
Rich vocabulary	_____	_____
Sentence Fluency		
Varied in size	_____	_____
Varied in structure	_____	_____
Conventions		
Appropriate punctuation	_____	_____
Correct grammar	_____	_____
Correct spelling	_____	_____
Presentation		
Typed in MLA format	_____	_____
Number of points		
Vocab words in essay (up to 5)	_____	_____
Total points/percentage	_____	_____

Andrew A

Mrs. Dettinger

High School Composition

28 September 2017

Dazzling Drones and Marvelous Money?

What if there was a way to make money and avoid the mind-numbing boredom of working at McDonald's? Well, you can, by starting your own home-based business! Although starting a business may seem frightening, it is rewarding to fill a need for a product or service (for example drone photography) in your community. Through effective planning and preparation, you'll be able to have a successful home-based business as a teen.

The first step to a successful home-based business is composing a business plan. In this plan, outline your product or service. Describe, for example, the aerial photography services offered, along with how much they would cost. After outlining your product or service, explain how your business will operate. Sketch out everything from how you'll send video and pictures to clients to when and where you can fly. Finally, construct financing and marketing strategies. Because a drone is an expensive item, a financing strategy must include how to pay for it and any other gear needed. Primarily, a well-written marketing strategy should comprise how you can sway potential customers. By drafting a top-notch business plan, you've made the first step on the journey to a successful home-based business!

Second, determine and purchase all of the supplies and equipment that your business needs. Think hard. Forgetting to buy a cord to connect a phone to the drone's controller would certainly embarrass you (and cause quite a quagmire!!) on your first job. Obviously, for a drone photography business, a high-quality drone (like a DJI Phantom 4) is absolutely essential, along with a smartphone or tablet to control it. Because a drone's battery dies all too quickly, purchasing a spare or two ensures you won't be dealing with irate clients who didn't get all the footage they wanted. Next, buy the necessary equipment. Clearly, an extra battery doesn't help at all if it's sitting in your Amazon cart. Carefully save all of the receipts to keep track of your expenses. Once all the requisite equipment has been bought, your home-based business will be ready for take off!

Powerful promotion will earn you eager customers. Churning out paper materials such as business cards and brochures, your printer moves your business along. After your printer hooks you up with a poster of your most spectacular aerial photo, hang it in a public place. The eyes of bored pedestrians will snap to the beautiful poster, and, of course, spot your prominently displayed contact information. While catching customers during their stroll down the street sounds pretty excellent, digital marketing smoothly reaches them as they reply to email, keep up with their friends, and even watch cat videos! A website overflowing with gorgeous drone videos effortlessly convinces potential clients that this guy is a magnificent photographer. Social media and business are besties! Promoted through social media like Facebook and Instagram, your stunning shots will definitely impress potential customers. Predictably, word-of-mouth promotes your business in a casual yet extremely effective way. Talk to your friends, teachers, grandparents, aunts, uncles and anybody else. The more people that know about your business the better! Also, fly that drone! The cacophony of the drone's rotors will promulgate your business by grabbing the attention of curious onlookers. Cogent marketing will lead to your first clients.

Although it takes effort, starting a home-based business as a teen is highly fulfilling. After all, who doesn't want some extra cash? Through starting a home-based business, you can avoid flipping those greasy burgers at McDonald's. Instead, you'll soar across the sky through the camera of a drone as you record breathtaking video and take spectacular photos.

Works Cited

Brookins, Amanda. "Starting a Home-based Business as a Teen" ehow Money, 2012. Demand Media. July 10, 2012. Web.

Lesson 3
Cause-Effect Essays

Quiz #2

Matching

1. _____ cacophony
2. _____ veracity
3. _____ quagmire
4. _____ cogent
5. _____ promulgate
6. _____ ubiquitous
7. _____ ineffable
8. _____ malevolent

A. a difficult situation
B. (seemingly) everywhere
C. tremendous noise, disharmonious sound
D. not able to express through words
E. wishing harm to others
F. truthfulness, accuracy
G. intellectually convincing
H. to proclaim or make known

Short Answer

9. What is the first step in writing a process essay?
_____

10. Draw and label each part of a graphic organizer for a process essay.

True or False

11. _____ You should always use the "writing process" when crafting an essay: research your topic, take notes, brainstorm ideas, write, edit, write, edit, and type.

12. _____ The body paragraphs of your essay should include evidence to support your points.

13. _____ A process essay explains something that happens in phases.

Lesson 3: The Cause-Effect Essay

Vocabulary for Lesson 3

Stupefy:

Tenuous:

Pugnacious:

A **cause-effect essay** is organized in one of two ways:

1. The thesis communicates a cause (such as a natural disaster) and the body paragraphs explain three effects.

2. The thesis communicates an effect (such as a war) and the body paragraphs explain three causes.

Study the graphic organizers on the next two pages.

Cause-Effect Essay (A)

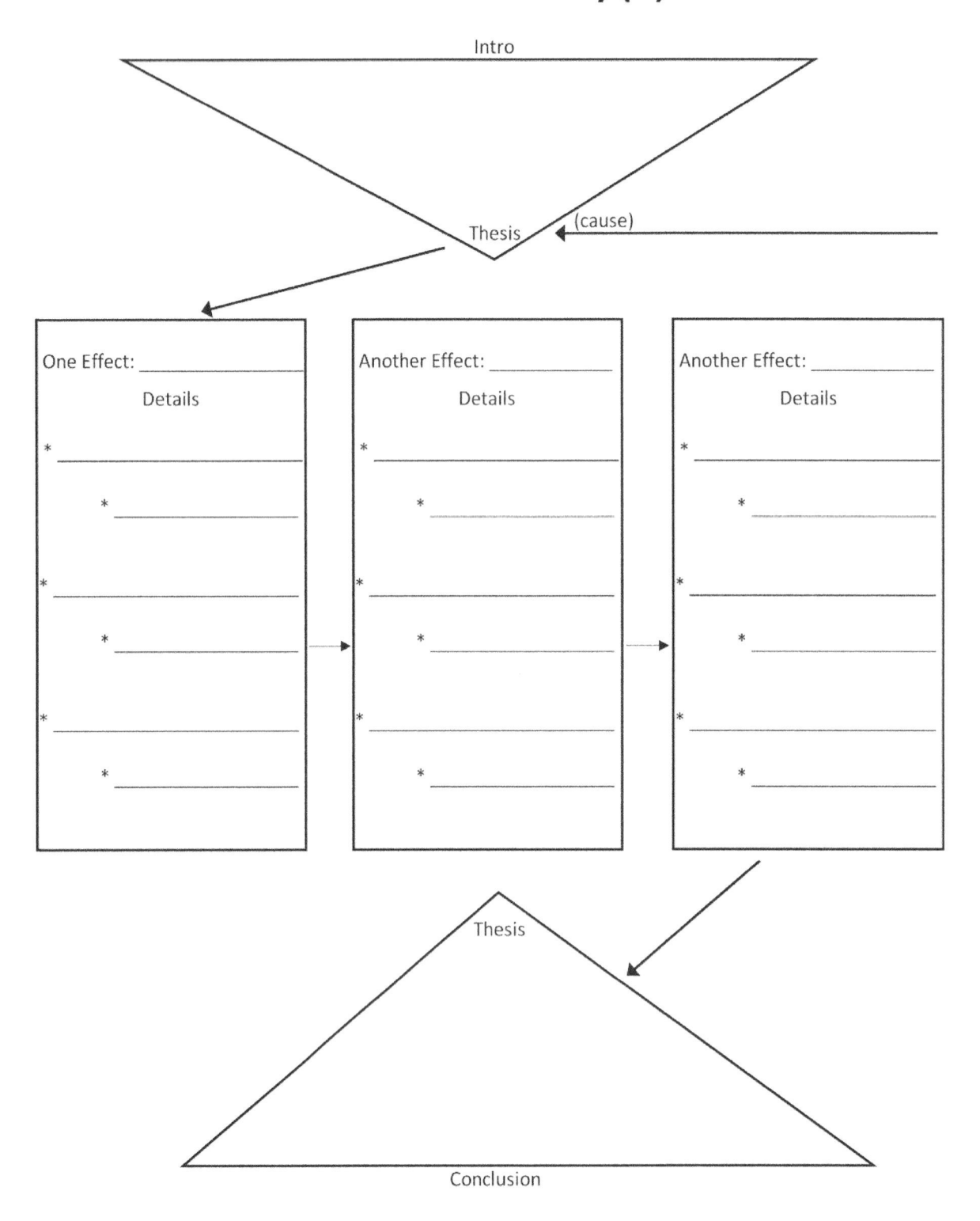

Intro

Thesis (cause)

One Effect: _____
Details
* _____
* _____
* _____
* _____
* _____

Another Effect: _____
Details
* _____
* _____
* _____
* _____
* _____

Another Effect: _____
Details
* _____
* _____
* _____
* _____
* _____

Thesis

Conclusion

©Powerhouse Educational Resources

Cause-Effect Essay (B)

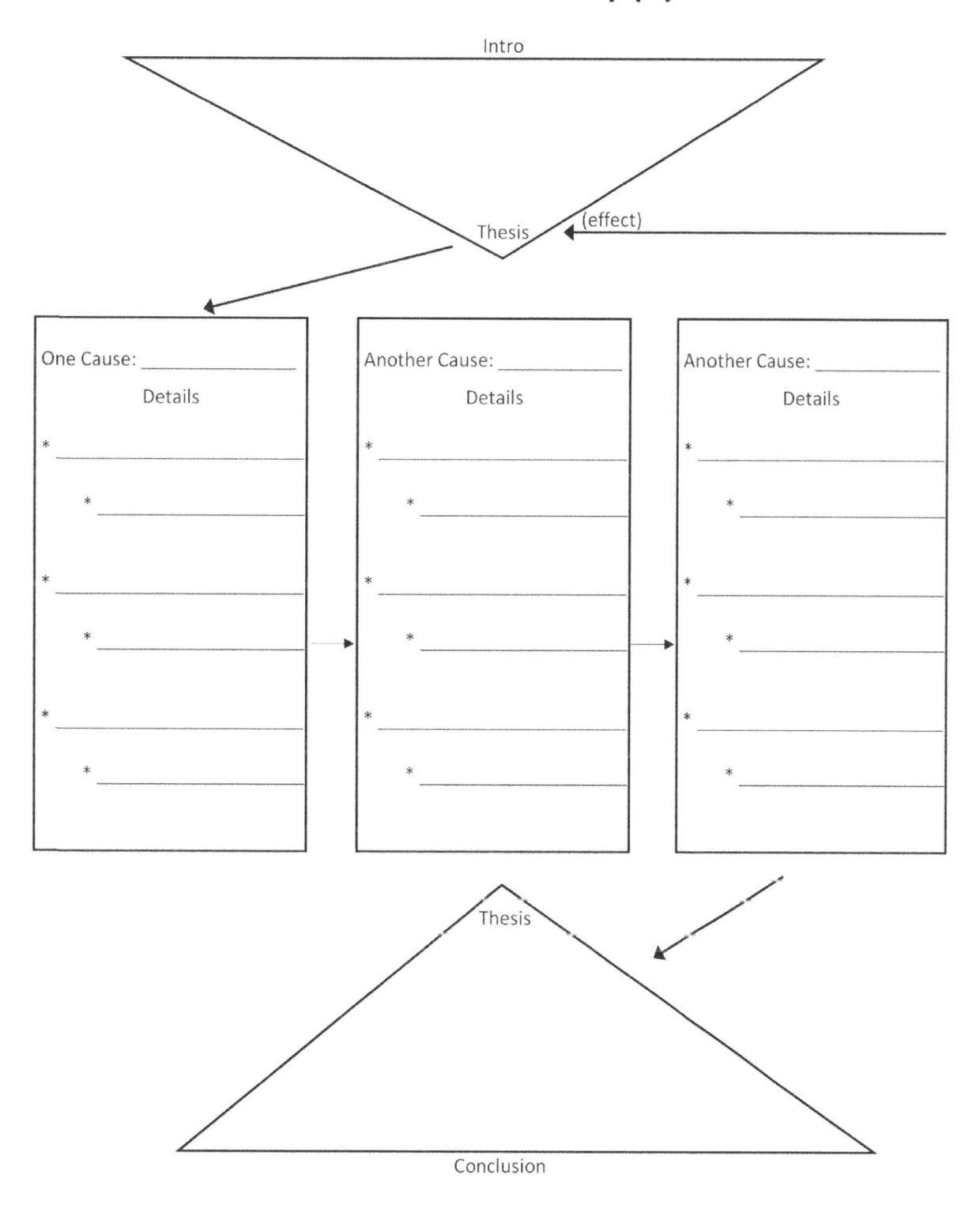

Intro

Thesis (effect)

One Cause: _____	Another Cause: _____	Another Cause: _____
Details	Details	Details
* _____	* _____	* _____
* _____	* _____	* _____
* _____	* _____	* _____
* _____	* _____	* _____
* _____	* _____	* _____

Thesis

Conclusion

©Powerhouse Educational Resources

Writing Introductions

1. Decide the attention-getter:
   - Startling statement
   - Story
   - Statistic
   - Quote
   - Query

2. Tie it in. Consider:
   - Why is this an important topic?
   - If using Graphic Organizer A, what causes led to the thesis statement?
   - If using Graphic Organizer B, is there a personal example or a primary source that can be used to develop the intro?

3. Thesis statement:
   - Two ways to organize
     - Thesis: Three ways internet has impacted society (organizer A)
     - Thesis: Three main causes of the Civil War (organizer B)

Sample Cause-Effect Introductions

In 1806, Napoleon Bonaparte was the most powerful and feared man in Europe. His French armies had rapidly conquered or subdued most of the land surrounding the Mediterranean, and were now preparing to launch a campaign against Great Britain. Many of his contemporaries thought him to be invincible. Though he was one of history's greatest military minds, Napoleon Bonaparte soon made three devastating mistakes that would spell the end of his massive empire. (Credit: James Oldenburg)

Graphic Organizer _____

"Then - have we no hope?" said Susan. When C.S. Lewis penned his famous novel-turned-movie, The Chronicles of Narnia: The Lion, the Witch, and the Wardrobe, *he conjured up a surreal world of talking creatures within the classic epic tale of good vs.*

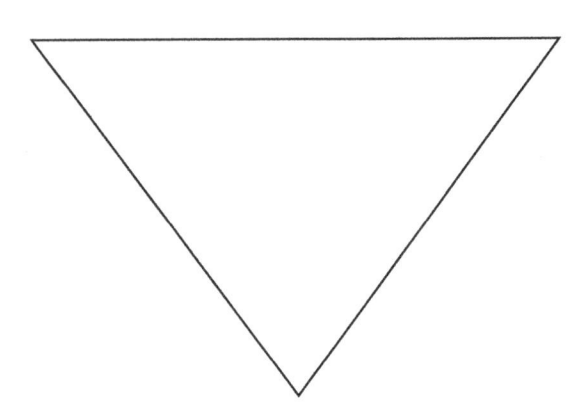

evil. The reader is carried with the tides of despair and triumph along with the characters - whether human, animal, or plant. In chapter 10, when Susan begs the "hope" question of Mrs. Beaver, the reader is relieved to hear her response, "'Course we've got a hope." This hope materializes in the form of an awe-inspiring lion named Aslan, the savior of the world of Narnia. Aslan's return to Narnia provides three signs which inspire hope for the Narnian residents and consequently, for the reader.

Graphic Organizer _____

Writing Conclusions

1. Recap thesis.

2. Summarize main points.
    Can refer to example or
    quote from intro.

3. Explain what *could have been* and/or what *ultimately happened*.

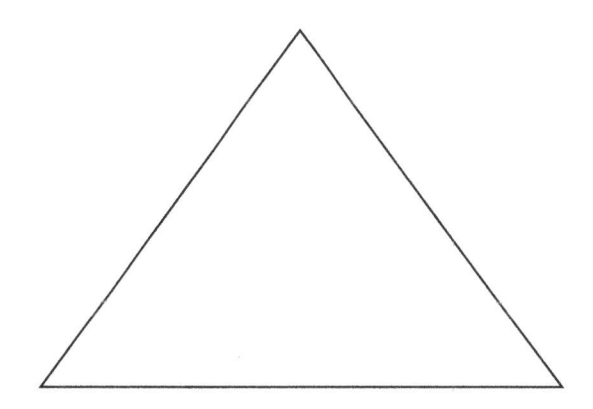

Sample Cause-Effect Conclusions

With three devastating mistakes, the Emperor of France lost everything he had gained. The Continental System was highly impractical, the Peninsular War was costly and indecisive, and the Invasion of Russia ended in disaster when winter came. Perhaps if Napoleon had somehow managed to tame his lust for glory and power he would have ruled Europe for the rest of his life. Instead, he was exiled to the remote island of Saint Helena in the southern Atlantic and spent the rest of his days writing his memoirs.

(Credit: James Oldenburg)

In sum, there are three effects of Aslan's presence in Narnia that inspire hope in the characters and consequently in the reader: the fulfilling of a prophecy, the weakening of the White Witch's magic, and the frustration of the White Witch as she struggles to maintain her dominion. Because Aslan is wholly good and emanates a lord-like presence throughout the book, the reader is encouraged to see the effects of his presence in Narnia. Ultimately, Aslan saves the kingdom by agreeing to die to pay for Edmund's transgressions. He then revives to win the battle of good and evil in Narnia, a battle in which the queen makes her last stand in her struggle to maintain her hold. She fails. Thus, the hopes of the Pavensies, the Narnian creatures, and the reader become realized. Good has triumphed over evil and Narnia is restored.

Cause-effect introductions and conclusions practically write themselves when you simply follow the formulas.

Sample introduction formula:
    Statistic
    Why relevant
    Thesis

Sample conclusion formula:
    Summarize thesis
    Recap main points
    What ultimately happened

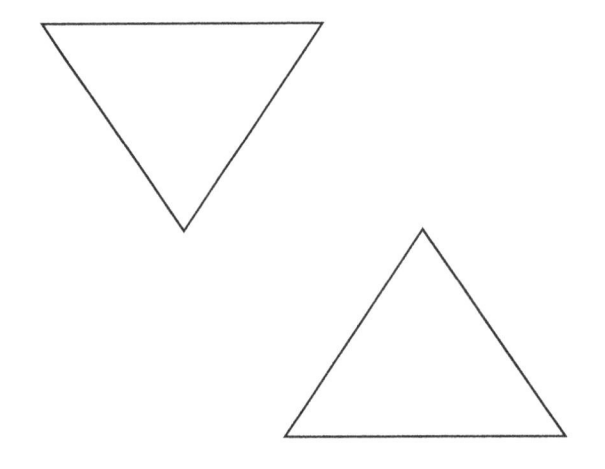

Writing the Cause-Effect Essay

Use the three simple steps for this essay:
1. Decide your graphic organizer.
2. Fill it in with your ideas.
3. Type it while researching your specific evidence.

Cause-Effect Essay Rubric

	Student	Teacher
Ideas		
Clearly defined thesis	_____	_____
Supportive examples of causes or effects	_____	_____
Depth of knowledge, insight	_____	_____
Holds reader's attention	_____	_____
Organization		
Paragraphs		
Intro (attention-getter, tie-in, thesis)	_____	_____
Body	_____	_____
Conclusion (summary of thesis, tie-in, closes)	_____	_____
Appropriate transitions	_____	_____
Voice		
Demonstrates writer's interest in topic	_____	_____
Uses creative expressions, images	_____	_____
Word Choice		
Powerful verbs	_____	_____
Specific nouns	_____	_____
Rich vocabulary	_____	_____
Sentence Fluency		
Varied in size	_____	_____
Varied in structure	_____	_____
Conventions		
Appropriate punctuation	_____	_____
Correct grammar	_____	_____
Correct spelling	_____	_____
Presentation		
Typed in MLA format	_____	_____
Number of points		
Vocab words in essay (up to 5)	_____	_____
Total points/percentage	_____	_____

Evan Scharnick

Mrs. Dettinger

High School Composition

23 February 2016

The Character of Master Samwise

Who do you think of as the hero of *The Lord of the Rings*? The natural answer is Frodo Baggins. He carries the Ring. He struggles and succeeds in resisting its power through the greatest of trials. But there is another who is equally integral to the success of the Fellowship of the Ring. Samwise Gamgee presents indispensable aid at all points throughout J.R.R. Tolkien's fantasy epic. Key to the support he furnishes are three exemplary aspects of his character.

First, Sam possesses **stupefying** loyalty which withstands all manner of thrashing. The center of his loyalty is Frodo. From the beginning, it is seen that Sam can't bear the thought that Frodo is going on a dangerous journey alone. The news makes him choke (*The Fellowship of the Ring* 70). As the tale unfolds further, Sam displays a power to resist the Ring unmatched by any but Frodo. When Frodo is incapacitated in the battle with Shelob, Sam is required to carry the Ring until he can rescue his master. He does this successfully, and even wears the Ring briefly. Despite the fact that it has driven mad some who have never even touched it, Sam faithfully defeats the Ring's temptations in the territory where its power is greatest. As Tolkien informs us in *The Return of the King*, "In that hour of trial it was the deep love for his master that helped most to hold him firm" (185).

Second, Sam possesses significant courage and determination, which is only increased as he faces greater challenges. When he first is told that he will go with Frodo, it is clear that he does not comprehend the situation. Instead, the decision elicits ignorant excitement at the possibility of meeting the elves. "'Me, sir!' cried Sam, springing up like a dog invited for a walk. 'Me go and see elves and all! Hooray!' he shouted, and then burst into tears" (*The Fellowship of the Ring* 70). However, as he begins to see more and more just how treacherous the quest really is, he does not waver, in great measure due to the aforementioned loyalty which he felt so strongly. Following many more steadily heightening perils, and hot on the heels of the Fellowship's most staggering tragedy, Sam sees a vision of mischief afoot in the Shire. Initially he is determined to turn back to stop what he has seen, but after receiving advice and struggling for a minute, he **promulgates** that "I'll go home by the long road with Mr. Frodo, or not at all" (*The Fellowship of the Ring* 407). A very long road later, Sam and Frodo have gotten so close to the end that they can literally see it, only to have the odds suddenly stack hopelessly against them. They must succeed or perish. While this realization might lead anyone to panic, Sam strives onward, simply acknowledging that "the perishing is more likely, and will be a lot easier anyway" (*The Return of the King* 182).

Third, while he may not have commanded it initially, Sam earns the respect of his comrades by his noble conduct. A clear sign of this is that he is permitted to accompany the Fellowship in the first place. After the Hobbits and Strider reach Rivendell, there is a surplus of heroes and warriors to send on the quest. It seems that a Hobbit gardener would only get in the way. Even so, Sam is the first to be told that he will embark with Frodo (*The Fellowship of the Ring* 304). At the end of the first book, when the Fellowship is broken and Frodo and Sam have gone alone into untold danger, the other companions could send at least one ally after them.

This would appear wisest. However, those who remain outside of Mordor trust both Frodo and Sam enough to leave them to the culmination of their journey, upon which the fate of the world depends. Once the quest is over and Frodo has sailed from the Grey Havens, we see in Appendix B that Sam is elected to seven consecutive seven-year terms as Mayor of the Shire, allowing him to oversee the recovery of the Shire following the tyranny of Saruman (*The Return of the King* 418).

The quest to destroy the Ring depends to a large extent on three positive character traits in Samwise Gamgee. He is fiercely loyal, gains great determination and courage, and receives well-deserved respect from those he helps. Imagine how the story would have turned if at any one of many points, Sam had not given, or had not been allowed to give, all that he had. Because of the support he provides, Sam ultimately proves himself to be the unsung hero of *The Lord of the Rings*.

Works Cited

Tolkien, J.R.R. *The Lord of the Rings: The Fellowship of the Ring.* New York: Ballantine Books, 1994. Print.

Tolkien, J.R.R. *The Lord of the Rings: The Return of the King.* New York: Ballantine Books, 1994. Print.

Tolkien, J.R.R. *The Lord of the Rings: The Two Towers.* New York: Ballantine Books, 1982. Print.

Lesson 4
Compare-Contrast Essays

Quiz #3

Matching

1. _____ quagmire   A. tremendous noise, disharmonious sound
2. _____ stupefy   B. not able to express through words
3. _____ promulgate   C. (seemingly) everywhere
4. _____ ineffable   D. wishing harm to others
5. _____ malevolent   E. intellectually convincing
6. _____ tenuous   F. truthfulness, accuracy
7. _____ ubiquitous   G. to proclaim or make known
8. _____ pugnacious   H. to astonish, make insensible
9. _____ cogent   I. a difficult situation
10. _____ veracity   J. quarrelsome, combative
11. _____ cacophony   K. having little substance or strength

Short Answer

12. Explain two different ways to organize a cause-effect essay.

_____

_____

Provide examples of the following:

13. The *opening* sentence of an essay about the Civil War.

_____

_____

14. A thesis statement for a cause-effect essay about the Civil War.

_____

_____

15. A closing sentence for the conclusion of a cause-effect essay about the Civil War.

_____

_____

Lesson 4: The Compare-Contrast Essay

Vocabulary for Lesson 4

Transient:

Usurp:

Manifold:

Compare: analyze similarities
Contrast: analyze differences

Ways to organize the compare-contrast essay:

    Block   **OR**   **Block**
        Block of similarities   Block about "X"
        Block of differences   Block about "Y"

    Point-by-Point
        Similarities and differences of three aspects

How the two methods compare:
- Same information presented
- Same introduction and conclusion

How the two methods contrast:
- Different organization of the body
- Four paragraphs rather than five

Compare-Contrast Essay (A)

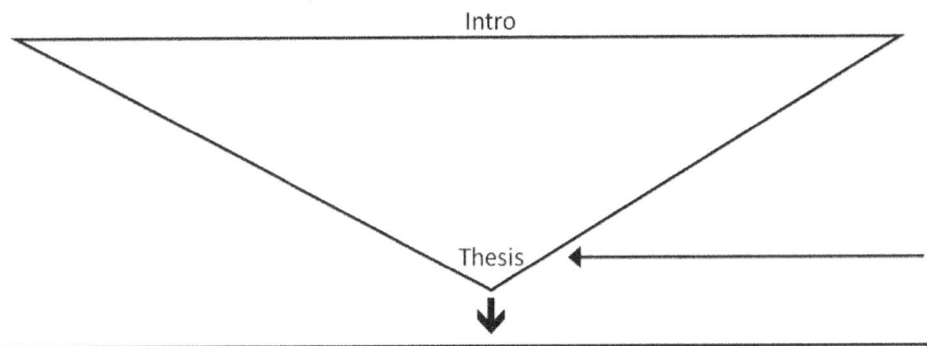

Intro

Thesis

One Similarity: _____	Another Similarity: _____
* _____ Ev. _____	* _____ Ev. _____
* _____ Ev. _____	* _____ Ev. _____
* _____ Ev. _____	* _____ Ev. _____

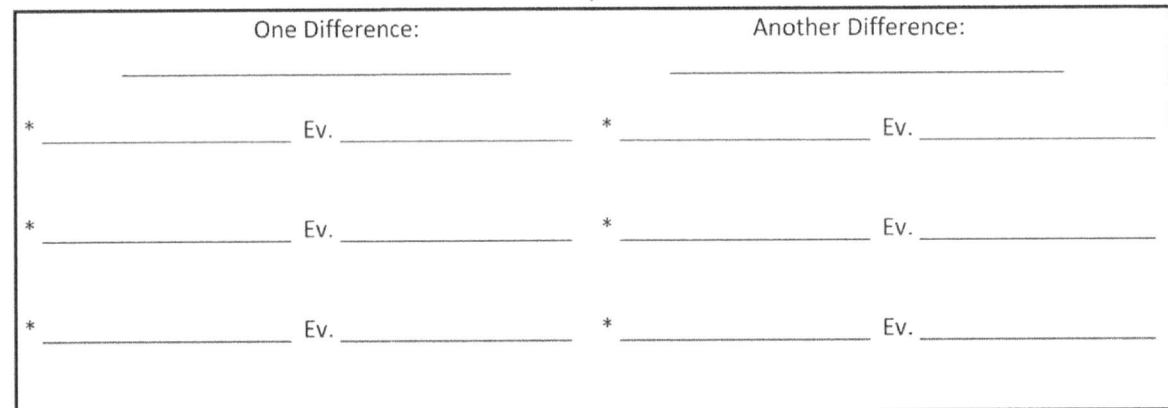

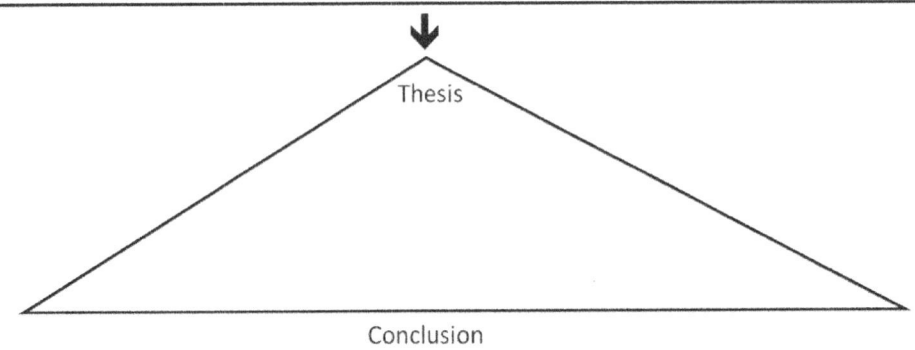

One Difference: _____	Another Difference: _____
* _____ Ev. _____	* _____ Ev. _____
* _____ Ev. _____	* _____ Ev. _____
* _____ Ev. _____	* _____ Ev. _____

Thesis

Conclusion

©Powerhouse Educational Resources

Compare-Contrast Essay (B)

Intro

Thesis

1st Aspect: _____

SAME: _____
Supporting Details
- _____
- _____

DIFFERENT: _____
Supporting Details
- _____
- _____

2nd Aspect: _____

SAME: _____
Supporting Details
- _____
- _____

DIFFERENT: _____
Supporting Details
- _____
- _____

3rd Aspect: _____

SAME: _____
Supporting Details
- _____
- _____

DIFFERENT: _____
Supporting Details
- _____
- _____

Thesis

Conclusion

©Powerhouse Educational Resources

Transition Words to Help Guide the Reader

Compare Words
Likewise
In comparison
Similarly
Besides
Also
In addition to
On one hand
In common
As well as

Contrast Words
However
In contrast
Instead
Although
Despite
Yet
On the other hand
Whereas
Nevertheless

Point-by-Point and Block
Thesis: Both cats and dogs can be excellent companions, but an appropriate choice depends on the pet owner's lifestyle, finances, and household accommodations.

Point-by-Point	Block	Block
P1: Lifestyle *Cats: can be alone all day. *Dogs: can be alone all day but need to be let out at night.	**P1: Similarities** *Lifestyle: can be alone all day. *Cost: food and vet care	**P1: Cats** *Lifestyle: can be alone all day. *Cost: food and vet care. *House accom: don't need much space.
P2: Cost *Cats: food and vet care *Dogs: food and vet care	**P2: Differences** *Lifestyles: dogs need to be let out at night. * Cost: cats cost more $ *Household: cats don't need much space, dogs often need yard/fence.	**P2: Dogs** *Lifestyle: alone all day, but let out at night. *Cost: food & vet care. *House Accom: often need yard/fence
P3: House Accommodations *Cats: don't need much space. *Dogs: often need yard/fence.		

Point-by-Point and Block
Thesis in Conclusion: When adopting a pet, a prospective owner must consider the lifestyle, finances, and household accommodations their furry companion would require.

Sample Compare-Contrast Intro and Conclusion (Organizer_____)

A God of Justice or of Grace?

Les Miserables is the poignant story of ex-convict Jean Valjean who turns from a life of bitterness towards God and society to a life characterized by grace and self-sacrifice. Inspector Javert is Valjean's counterpart in the story and is characterized by a determination to uphold justice through a fastidious application of the laws of the French government. Throughout their lives, Javert and Valjean experienced the tension between grace and justice. According to the Merriam-Webster dictionary, grace is unmerited assistance that is given to an individual who did nothing to deserve it; justice is the administration of the law, especially through assigning merited punishment. This presents a seeming paradox. How can justice be satisfied when grace is given? <u>Manifold</u> circumstances presented the paradox between grace and justice to both men, who finished their lives with opposite outcomes. When you compare and contrast the lives of Javert and Valjean, you see three similar aspects that resulted in dissimilar mindsets and actions that are worth examining.

    The first aspect of Javert and Valjean's life that influenced them in different ways is their background of crime. (...)

    The second aspect of Javert and Valjean's life, the basis for their decisions and actions, is their view of God. (...)

    The third aspect of Javert and Valjean's life that displays their different mindsets in action is their role in society. (...)

    In sum, three similar aspects in the lives of Javert and Valjean produced dissimilar mindsets and actions: their background of crime, their view of God, and their role in society. The fundamental difference in the actions of both men lie in their attitudes towards grace and justice. Valjean saw his inadequacy to meet the demands of the law and therefore he deserved justice, but received grace. Javert on the other hand, saw that justice must be served and tried to satisfy the demands of the law apart from any grace. The apostle Paul says in Ephesians 2:8-9, "for by grace you have been saved through faith. And this is not your own doing; it is the gift of God, not a result of works, so that no one may boast" (English Standard Version). Javert had no category for grace. He could not comprehend the coexistence of grace and justice, a seeming paradox that propelled him to the point of suicide. In contrast, at the end of Valjean's life, after being hunted by the law and haunted by his own sin, he dies knowing that by Christ's death, justice was satisfied. He was forgiven. Javert's faith was in himself, while Valjean's faith was in God.

(Credit: Jacy K.)

Compare-Contrast Essay Rubric

	Student	Teacher
Ideas		
Clearly defined thesis	___	___
Supportive examples	___	___
Depth of knowledge, insight	___	___
Holds reader's attention	___	___
Organization		
Paragraphs		
Intro (attention-getter, tie-in, thesis)	___	___
Body (clearly point-by-point or clearly block)	___	___
Conclusion (summary of thesis, tie-in, closure)	___	___
Appropriate transitions	___	___
Voice		
Demonstrates writer's interest in topic	___	___
Uses creative expressions, images	___	___
Word Choice		
Powerful verbs	___	___
Specific nouns	___	___
Rich vocabulary	___	___
Sentence Fluency		
Varied in size	___	___
Varied in structure	___	___
Conventions		
Appropriate punctuation	___	___
Correct grammar	___	___
Correct spelling	___	___
Presentation		
Typed in MLA format	___	___
Number of points		
Vocab words in essay (up to 5)	___	___
Total points/percentage	___	___

Merissa E

Mrs. Dettinger

High School Composition

18 October 2017

The Lord and the Slave

Mara, Daughter of the Nile is the captivating story of a young girl named Mara and her struggle to gain freedom from slavery. The plot thickens when the young nobleman, Lord Sheftu, joins the scene. These two complex characters are in constant conflict throughout the story, both within themselves and with each other. Although Mara and Lord Sheftu come from vastly different backgrounds, they share a common desire for freedom from the bondage they're in. The book promulgates how they seek freedom and, in the end, both attain it.

Both Mara and Lord Sheftu share the desire for freedom. Mara craves the freedom of not being a slave and Lord Sheftu desires Egypt to be free from Pharaoh's sister, who has usurped the power of the throne. These two young people are willing to take extreme risks to gain this freedom. Besides this shared desire for freedom, the two are also being manipulated and used as pawns in a quagmire of political strife. Mara is being used by her master, Lord Nahereh, as a spy to seek out the messenger of the rebellion led by Lord Sheftu. Lord Sheftu, thinking Mara a mere runaway slave, enlists her in his service as the messenger for the rebellion. Thus, Lord Sheftu is being used by Mara without knowing it and Mara is being used by Lord Nahereh. They both struggle to keep their wits about them and stay one step ahead in the dangerous game they're playing.

Despite their similarities, Mara and Lord Sheftu have manifold differences in their goals for life. Although Mara would rather die than be a slave, her desire to be free from slavery compels her to take whatever risks necessary to attain it. She plays the dangerous game of serving two "masters," Lord Nahereh and Lord Sheftu. Thus, whichever one is successful she plans to benefit from. Mara is willing to sacrifice nearly everything for personal freedom, including playing with the very fate of Egypt. As stated in chapter sixteen, "she hoped he would never know how fast and loose she had played with the fate of Egypt and his king" (180). The "he" in this quote refers to Lord Sheftu, who is head of the rebellion that wants to place the rightful Pharaoh on the throne. In contrast to Mara, who seeks freedom for herself, Lord Sheftu is willing to risk everything including his life and freedom for Egypt. He robs the grave of a deceased Pharaoh and nearly dies in the process. For Lord Sheftu, whatever sacrifice it takes is worth it to set the rightful Pharaoh on the throne. The saving of Egypt is worth the risk of life, freedom, and failure. Although both Lord Sheftu and Mara pursue freedom, their means of attaining it and for whom it benefits are extremely different. Another difference between them is their background. The only life Mara knows is that of a slave. Mara views the world through the eyes of one who merely wants to gain from it and profit herself. Everyone who comes into her life goes out of it without any meaning or emotional attachment. Lord Sheftu, on the other hand, grew up as a nobleman, attended school, and met Thutmose (the rightful Pharaoh) at a young age. The two became best friends and their friendship influences the rest of Lord Sheftu's life. In contrast, Mara has never had someone take a place of friendship in her heart.

In summary, the two main characters of the book *Mara, Daughter of the Nile* both desperately seek freedom and although they are uniquely different they share the same fierce determination and motivation to achieve their goal. Mara and Lord Sheftu are both being used and manipulated while they pursue their cause. They are from extremely different backgrounds and have contrasting goals for life. The pursuit of their individual goals brings Mara and Lord Sheftu together, despite their pugnacious attitude towards each other. The two conflicting, albeit similar, characters both take hazardous and dangerous risks to chase freedom. In the end, they each gain the freedom they have so long coveted.

Works Cited

McGraw, Eloise Jarvis. "Chapter Sixteen." *Mara, Daughter of the Nile*, Puffin Books, 1985.

Lesson 5
Editorial Essays

Quiz #4

Matching

1. _____ usurp
2. _____ stupefy
3. _____ promulgate
4. _____ manifold
5. _____ malevolent
6. _____ cogent
7. _____ ubiquitous
8. _____ pugnacious
9. _____ tenuous
10. _____ veracity
11. _____ cacophony
12. _____ transient
13. _____ quagmire
14. _____ ineffable

A. wishing harm to others
B. not able to express through words
C. (seemingly) everywhere
D. passing through briefly; passing into and out of existence
E. intellectually convincing
F. diverse, varied
G. to proclaim or make known
H. to astonish, make insensible
I. a difficult situation
J. to seize by force or take possession without right
K. having little substance or strength
L. quarrelsome, combative
M. truthfulness, accuracy
N. tremendous noise, disharmonious sound

Fill in the blank.

15. A general term for an essay meant to inform the reader: _____.

16. An essay about the similarities and differences between the U.S. Revolution and the French Revolution is a _____ essay.

17. An essay describing the effects of a medical discovery is a _____ essay.

18. A general term for an essay that attempts to sway the reader toward the author's point of view: _____.

19. An essay that explains the stages of meiosis is a _____ essay.

20. In the space below, draw and label two simple graphic organizer templates, one representing a point-by-point compare-contrast essay, and one representing a block method compare-contrast essay.

Point-by-Point   **Block**

Lesson 5: The Editorial

Vocabulary for Lesson 5

Zenith:

Neophyte:

_____

Editorial's purpose: to persuade the reader to _____
_____
- Can use humor, drama, passion, emotion, figurative language.

Introduction: present a problem/conflict to gain reader's interest and alignment.
- Thesis should be current, relevant, simple, and debatable.

Body: only need to present YOUR side well (opinionated but well-supported).

Conclusion:

- Briefly restate reasons/supports.
- Make reader think
- Restate opinion or call to specific action.
  - Heart of an editorial – last thought for the reader.

Notes about the editorial:
- Be passionate about your topic. Believe in it.
- Avoid overuse of "I."
- Base evidence on fact, not hearsay or opinion.
- Newspaper editorials are many small paragraphs. Editorial *essays* will follow a more typical essay structure.

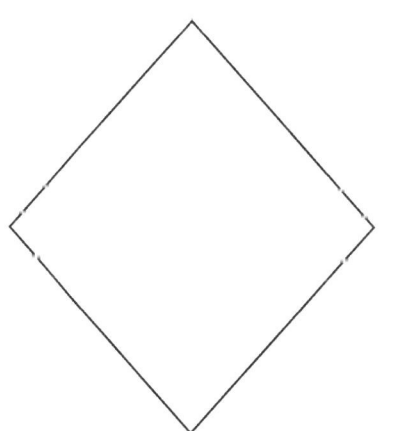

Editorial Essay

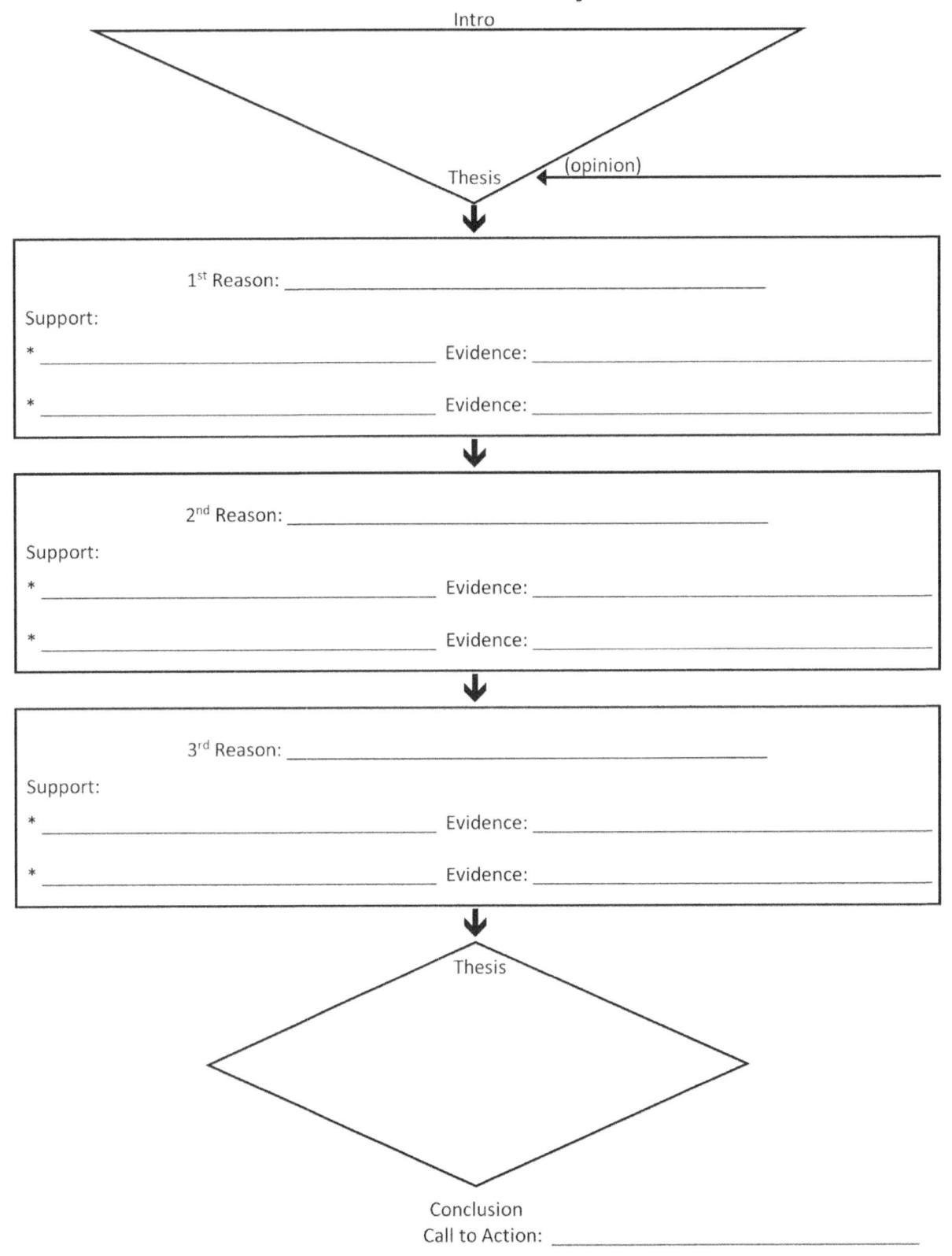

Intro

Thesis ←―― (opinion) _____

1st Reason: _____
Support:
* _____ Evidence: _____
* _____ Evidence: _____

2nd Reason: _____
Support:
* _____ Evidence: _____
* _____ Evidence: _____

3rd Reason: _____
Support:
* _____ Evidence: _____
* _____ Evidence: _____

Thesis

Conclusion
Call to Action: _____

©Powerhouse Educational Resources

Editorial Exercise

Choose one of the two articles from the following pages to complete the exercise. (They are not MLA formatted.)

Title of Editorial:_____

1. What is the bottom-line opinion for the editorial? Where in the article do you find this?

2. How did the editorial grab your attention?

3. Was the thesis clearly stated in the introduction? Was it phrased the same as in the conclusion? Which was clearer?

4. Can you identify the supporting evidence for the writer's opinion in each of the body paragraphs? Is the organization of the writer's ideas comparable to the editorial graphic organizer or is it different?

5. Identify a few key $10 words and idiomatic expressions found in the editorial.

6. Does the editorial lead you to strongly agree or disagree with its author or cause you to want to take action on the issue?

An essay by Miriam Gold, age 14, a top 10 finalist in the 2016 New York Times' "Learning Network" Editorial Essay Contest.

It's Time for Teens to Vote

At sixteen years old, Jack Andraka discovered an inexpensive method to test for pancreatic cancer. At just fifteen, Louis Braille invented the Braille writing system, allowing the blind to read and write. Additionally, Malala Yousafzai was seventeen when she won the Nobel Peace Prize for promoting women's education in Pakistan. These teens show themselves to be innovators and inspirers, their work rivaling the achievements of our most celebrated adults. However, even with the potential that every teen holds, they are denied a voice in who governs their own country. As a politically aware high school student, I should be allowed to vote at sixteen in the November 2016 election because my opinion is no less valid than the adults who vote.

Throughout history, restricted voting has been a way for the government to stifle the voices of those they did not want to hear. In 1870, blacks were finally given the right to vote; and in 1920, Congress gave voting rights to women. Finally, Americans understood that no matter what group someone belonged to, their right to vote should be protected — except one group, teens. Through unfair voting law, teens are told that the fundamental rights of all Americans do not apply to them.

Many who deny teens' rights to vote believe teens will make uninformed decisions that will hurt the country. Although many teens may seem not to care about voting now, this could easily be changed. An extremely effective ways to increase voting interest is "to inoculate [teens] with a significant dose of meaningful responsibility and authority" (Epstein 17). If students are given the responsibility of a vote that will affect their life, most will become more invested in electing the best candidate.

Although teens are not extended the rights of adults, they are still burdened with the responsibilities. In many states, "A child, defined as a person under age 18, can be tried as an adult if the child was age 14 or older at the time of the offense" ("How"). If our society believes teens can handle the burden of adult responsibility, why are they believed undeserving of adult rights?

Not only do teens deserve the right to vote, their votes would prove constructive to society. Research shows political involvement by teens to "trickle up" to their parents, increasing voter turnout, and, "Empirical evidence suggests that the earlier in life a voter casts their first ballot, the more likely they are to develop voting as a habit" ("Lower"). Low voter turnout is only worsening, but teen voting could help turn this issue around because countless teenagers like myself would be proud to fill out the ballots deciding our country's future.

Works Cited

Belluck, Pam. "Sixteen Candles, but Few Blazing a Trail to the Ballot Box." The New York Times. The New York Times, 26 Aug. 2007. Web. 24 Mar. 2016.

"Chapter 12. Political Socialization and Civic Competence." Political Attitudes and Democracy in Five Nations The Civic Culture (2006): n. pag. Web. 24 Mar. 2016.

Epstein, Robert. Teen 2.0: Saving Our Children and Families From the Torment of Adolescence. Fresno, CA: Quill Driver/Word Dancer, 2010. Print.

Giacomo, Carol. "A Nobel Peace Prize for Malala Yousafzai." The New York Times n.d.: n. pag. Taking Note: A Nobel Peace Prize for Malala Yousafzai Comments. The New York Times, 10 Oct. 2014. Web. 24 Mar. 2016.

"How Are Juveniles Tried as Adults?" Ohio State Bar Association. www.ohiobar.org, 21 Sept. 2015. Web. 24 Mar. 2016.

Kaiman, Jonathan, Amanda Holpuch, David Smith, Jonathan Watts and Alexandra Topping. "Beyond Malala: Six Teenagers Changing the World." The Guardian. Guardian News and Media, 18 Oct. 2013. Web. 24 Mar. 2016.

"Lower the Voting Age — FairVote." FairVote. N.p., n.d. Web. 24 Mar. 2016.

"Why October Is Youth History Month." Youth History Month. Pro-Youth Pages, 2007. Web. 24 Mar. 2016.

An essay by Jason Schnall, age 16, a top 10 finalist in the 2018 New York Times' "Learning Network" Editorial Essay Contest.

The 4th R: Real Life

Who's to blame for ballooning credit card debt and student loans? The public education system, perhaps. American high school students can recite Shakespeare's sonnets, derive advanced calculus theorems, and explain the Chinese spheres of influence. Yet these same students know little to nothing about economics and personal finance. They know of income tax only as the fifth square on the Monopoly board.

Currently, only five states — Alabama, Missouri, Tennessee, Utah and Virginia — require personal finance courses for high school students. The results speak for themselves: four of these states rank in the top 20 of best average credit card debt. This is a logical correlation. Learning about debt will help someone stay out of it. Yet economists continually blame consumerism and tactics of credit card companies rather than addressing the cause: a fundamental void in our education system.

When students graduate high school, they are thrust into adulthood, whether they join the workforce or pursue higher education. They assume immense financial responsibilities almost immediately. How can the government expect 19-year-olds to complete tax forms if they've never learned about them in school? Young adults who lack basic knowledge of economics and personal finance are vulnerable to fraud, debt, commercialism and worse.

Ideally, parents with lifelong experience would teach their children about personal finance. But, 61 percent of parents only discuss money when prompted by their children. The average American parent lacks the knowledge necessary to teach this information, as many of them live in severe debt themselves, including the 32 percent of U.S. households that carry credit card debt.

The solution? A required course — Personal Finance and the Modern Economy — taught to second-semester high school seniors. It's vital that students learn basic information about taxes, insurance, mortgages, credit, loans, personal banking, consumerism and the stock market before they are forced to learn it the hard way.

Financial literacy should not be a privilege reserved for children of the Wall Street elite. It is a skill that must be taught, just as vital in today's economy as reading, writing and arithmetic. So why do we keep treating it like an elective?

Works Cited

"Average Credit Card Debt in America: 2017 Facts & Figures." ValuePenguin, ValuePenguin, 21 March 2018.

Desjardins, Jeff. "Chart: Are Today's Students Prepared to Make Financial Decisions?" Visual Capitalist, 29 Sept. 2017.

"T. Rowe Price: Parents Are Likely To Pass Down Good And Bad Financial Habits To Their Kids." T.Rowe Price, 23 March 2017.

Warren, Mathew R. "Financial Literacy Class Offers Skills Not Taught in School." The New York Times, 27 Jan. 2012.

Practice

Suppose your state legislature is considering changing the legal driving age. Your assignment is to write an editorial ***introduction and conclusion*** based on one of the following positions.

"The legal driving age should be raised to 18."
OR
"The legal driving age should NOT be raised to 18."

Optional Statistics/Data/Evidence

Web article: "Should we Raise the Legal Driving Age?"
From: Drive-safely.net February 19, 2015. www.drive-safely.net/driving-age/

Teen Driving is Deadly
It's an unfortunate truth, but auto accidents are the leading cause of death among teenagers. A 16 year old is almost twice as likely to die in a car crash than a 30 year old. And with new issues such as cell phone driving, texting while driving, and other forms of distracted driving, there is good reason to debate this issue. If we can take the most dangerous drivers off the road, we will not only save the lives of young adults, but we will also make the roadways safer for everyone else.

But Driving is Deadly for all Age Groups
What's interesting is the leading cause of death for 15 to 24 year olds is auto accidents. They are the only age group where this is true. However, car crashes are the leading cause of accidental death in all age groups over 4 years old! Let's face it, 15 to 24 year olds aren't plagued with disease and sickness like older folks are. So it's only natural that their leading cause of death will be accidental, and will also be the leading accidental death for nearly every age group. So the stats aren't exactly cut and dry.

Is it Age or Inexperience? Consider These Points
Is age really the biggest factor to consider? If we raise the legal driving age to, say, 17 years old, wouldn't 17 year olds have the highest accident rate simply due to lack of experience? Many argue that our decision making skills aren't fully developed at 16 (the legal age at which a license can actually be obtained). However, this is mostly unsubstantiated evidence and since every person develops differently, a blanketed law is going to punish those who are ready.

I'm a truck driver and see this with new truckers. The legal age to receive a commercial driver's license is 18 years old, but most don't obtain their commercial driver's license until after the age of 21. The most dangerous truck drivers on the road are those with under 2 years of experience, regardless of age. It's likely that if we simply raise the driving age, we will only shift the "problem drivers" to a higher age bracket.

Web article: "States Urged To Raise The Driving Age"

From: CBS/AP September 10, 2008. www.cbsnews.com/news/states-urged-to-raise-the-driving-age/

More than 5,000 U.S. teens die each year in car crashes. The rate of crashes, fatal and nonfatal, per mile driven for 16-year-old drivers is almost 10 times the rate for drivers ages 30 to 59, according to the National Highway Safety Administration. Many industrialized countries in Europe and elsewhere have a driving age of 17 or 18.

Barbara Harsha, executive director of the Governors Highway Safety Association, said she welcomes a debate on raising the driving age - as do many who deal with public health.

"Getting the highest of the high-risk drivers away from the wheel probably isn't a bad idea," said Dr. Barbara Gaines, trauma director at Children's Hospital of Pittsburgh of UPMC.

Not surprisingly, a lot of teens hate the idea.

"I would really be upset because I've waited so long to drive," said Diamante White, a 16-year-old in Reading, Pa., who got her permit in July. She said learning to drive is a "growing-up experience."

Many parents agree. They also like not having to chauffeur their teens to school, sporting events and any number of other places.

"Do we really want our kids dependent upon parents for virtually everything until they go to college, can vote and serve their country?" asked Margaret Menotti, a mother in Uxbridge, Mass. She argued that keeping teens from driving would only make them less responsible. Some parents also find it ironic that this conversation is happening just as a group of college presidents have proposed lowering the drinking age to 18.

This page is for your Lesson 5B practice. You may write your official editorial essay on this topic or choose another one.

Should the Legal Driving Age Be Raised to 18?

First sentence of first point:

First sentence of second point:

First sentence of third point:

Editorial Essay Rubric

	Student	Teacher

Ideas
Clearly, valid, current thesis   _____   _____
Well-supported examples   _____   _____
Convincing   _____   _____
Holds reader's attention   _____   _____

Organization
Paragraphs
   Intro (attention-getter, tie-in, thesis)   _____   _____
   Body   _____   _____
   Conclusion (clear call to action or belief) _____   _____
Appropriate transitions   _____   _____

Voice
Demonstrates writer's passion for topic   _____   _____
Uses creative expressions, images   _____   _____

Word Choice
Powerful verbs   _____   _____
Specific nouns   _____   _____
Rich vocabulary   _____   _____

Sentence Fluency
Varied in size   _____   _____
Varied in structure   _____   _____

Conventions
Appropriate punctuation   _____   _____
Correct grammar   _____   _____
Correct spelling   _____   _____

Presentation
Typed in MLA format   _____   _____

Number of points
Vocab words in essay (up to 5)   _____   _____
Total points/percentage   _____   _____

Paige Reardon

Mrs. Dettinger

High School Composition

19 February 2018

Gun Control Doesn't Help Anyone

Gun law advocates all around the United States are pushing for the enforcement of gun control with the hopes of making a safer country. But do gun laws really help stop armed robberies and mass shootings? Does having fewer guns make America a safer place, or is it just giving the people a feeling of complacency? The Second Amendment is a freedom that we, as American Citizens, have enjoyed since the foundation of this country, but the good intentions of gun laws are threatening to infringe upon our rights to "keep and bear arms" (*U.S. Constitution*). It's disheartening to see today's Americans pushing to eradicate the rights that many of our forefathers died for. By taking away this freedom, gun laws are not helping anyone.

Contrary to popular belief, gun control does not help prevent acts of gun violence. Both Australia and the United Kingdom have recently enforced stricter gun laws, so most people would assume they have experienced less gun violence. This, however, is not the case. The 2017 data gathered by statistician Leah Libersco shows that neither country has fewer mass shootings or other gun related crime under the new laws. (Haskins). And take Jamaica, for example. They have extremely rigid gun laws, yet the murder rate there is close to the highest on the planet. But that wasn't always so. "In 1962… Jamaica had a murder rate of 3.9 per 100,000 population, one of the lowest in the world" says Dean Weingarten. In 2012, the murder rates were calculated at 45.1 per 100,000, 11 times greater than in 1962. What could have possibly happened between

45.1 per 100,000, 11 times greater than in 1962. What could have possibly happened between 1962 and 2012? The government imposed complete gun prohibition (Weingarten). Yes, it is an extreme example, but I believe the outcome speaks for itself. No good came out of Jamaica banning guns, so what good will come out of harsher gun laws in America?

Not only do gun laws not affect the amount of violence in the places they're enforced, but they just make it harder for innocent, trustworthy citizens to defend themselves. Restricting and harshly regulating who can own a gun unavoidably makes it harder for law-abiding citizens to have the means to protect themselves. Firearms are used 2.5 million times a year (6850 times a day) by U.S. citizens in self defense. Therefore, guns are used over 80 times more to protect lives than to take them. "As many as 200,000 women use a gun every year to defend themselves against sexual abuse" says the GOA. The veracity of these facts helps prove that guns essentially save more lives than they take, and prevent more injuries than they inflict (Gun Owners). The positive obviously outnumbers the negative here.

Aside from all of this, the most obvious reason why gun control is not effective is that no matter what types of laws or regulations are made, criminals will always find a way to get their hands on a gun. It's as simple as that. The University of Pittsburgh did a study they called "Who's Responsible for Gun Crime?" In this study, led by epidemiologist Anthony Fabio of Pittsburgh's Graduate School of Public Health, researchers teamed with the Pittsburgh Bureau of Police to trace the origins of 893 firearms that had been recovered from crime scenes in 2008. They found that 79% of the time, the perpetrator was not the legal owner of the gun, but rather, they were carrying a firearm owned by someone else (Ingraham). This information may stupefy some, but we must understand that criminals will be criminals. Gun laws and regulations won't stop people from stealing and using illegal firearms. Perpetrators are already breaking the law, so what's to stop them from breaking gun laws? Enforcing gun control would literally just give malevolent crooks more laws they will surely disregard.

    Putting all of the evidence in light points towards the egregious fact that gun control won't do the job in stopping violent crime. Other countries have tried and failed. On the other hand, something gun control will succeed in is giving criminals more laws to break, and making it harder for law-abiding Americans to own firearms that will defend lives and property. All of this proves that gun control simply won't help anyone.

Works Cited

Gun Owners of America. "Fact Sheet: Guns Save Lives." gunownersofamerica.org. October 16, 2008. GOA. February 19, 2018. Web.

Haskins, Justin. "We Don't Need Gun Control to Stop Mass Shootings." townhall.com. November 6, 2017. Townhall. February 15, 2018. Web.

Ingraham, Christopher. "New Evidence Confirms What Gun Rights Advocates Have Said For a Long Time About Crime." washingtonpost.com. July 27, 2016. The Washington Post. February 15, 2018. Web.

U.S. Constitution. Amend. XXII, Sec. 2.

Weingarten, Dean. "Jamaica: Gun Laws and Murder Rates." ammoland.com. December 4, 2015. Ammoland Inc. February 19, 2018. Web.

Lesson 6
Problem-Solution Essay

Quiz #5

Matching

1. _____ malevolent
2. _____ ineffable
3. _____ ubiquitous
4. _____ promulgate
5. _____ cogent
6. _____ quagmire
7. _____ veracity
8. _____ cacophony
9. _____ stupefy
10. _____ tenuous
11. _____ pugnacious
12. _____ transient
13. _____ usurp
14. _____ manifold
15. _____ zenith
16. _____ neophyte

A. to astonish, make insensible
B. quarrelsome, combative
C. having little substance or strength
D. tremendous noise, disharmonious sound
E. (seemingly) everywhere
F. someone who is young or inexperienced
G. not able to express through words
H. to proclaim or make known
I. passing through briefly; passing into and out of existence
J. diverse, varied
K. wishing harm to others
L. a difficult situation
M. truthfulness, accuracy
N. the highest point, the culminating point
O. intellectually convincing
P. to seize by force or take possession without right

Short Answer

17. Is an editorial essay expository or persuasive? _____

18. Give an example of an editorial essay thesis.
_____
_____

19. Below, draw the shape that would represent an editorial's conclusion.

20. Why is the editorial's conclusion shaped this way? Explain.
_____
_____

Lesson 6: The Problem-Solution Essay

Vocabulary for Lesson 6

Fetter:

Iconoclast:

Options for Organization
1. Thesis states problem and body provides three possible solutions.

2. Thesis states problem and proposes solution. Body provides three reasons for that solution and/or three ways to implement the solution.

VERY important to provide _____ _____.

Graphic Organizer A
Problem: Need money for college

Three possible solutions:
   1.)
   2.)
   3.)

Graphic Organizer B
Problem: Need money for college
Solution: Gap year

Three reasons to take a gap year:
   1.)
   2.)
   3.)

Problem-Solution Essay (A)

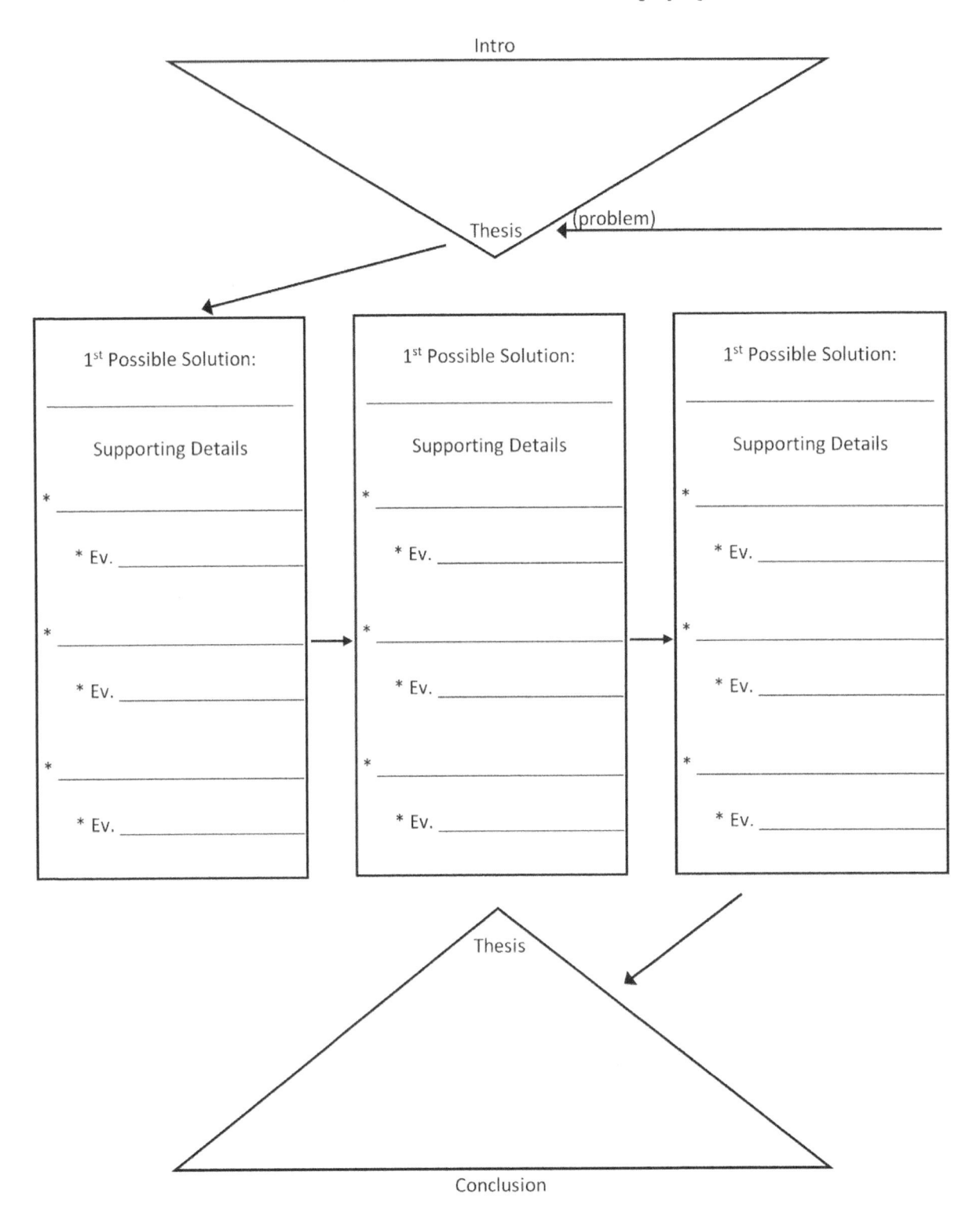

Intro

Thesis ← (problem)

1st Possible Solution: _____	1st Possible Solution: _____	1st Possible Solution: _____
Supporting Details	Supporting Details	Supporting Details
* _____	* _____	* _____
* Ev. _____	* Ev. _____	* Ev. _____
* _____	* _____	* _____
* Ev. _____	* Ev. _____	* Ev. _____
* _____	* _____	* _____
* Ev. _____	* Ev. _____	* Ev. _____

Thesis

Conclusion

©Powerhouse Educational Resources

Problem-Solution Essay (B)

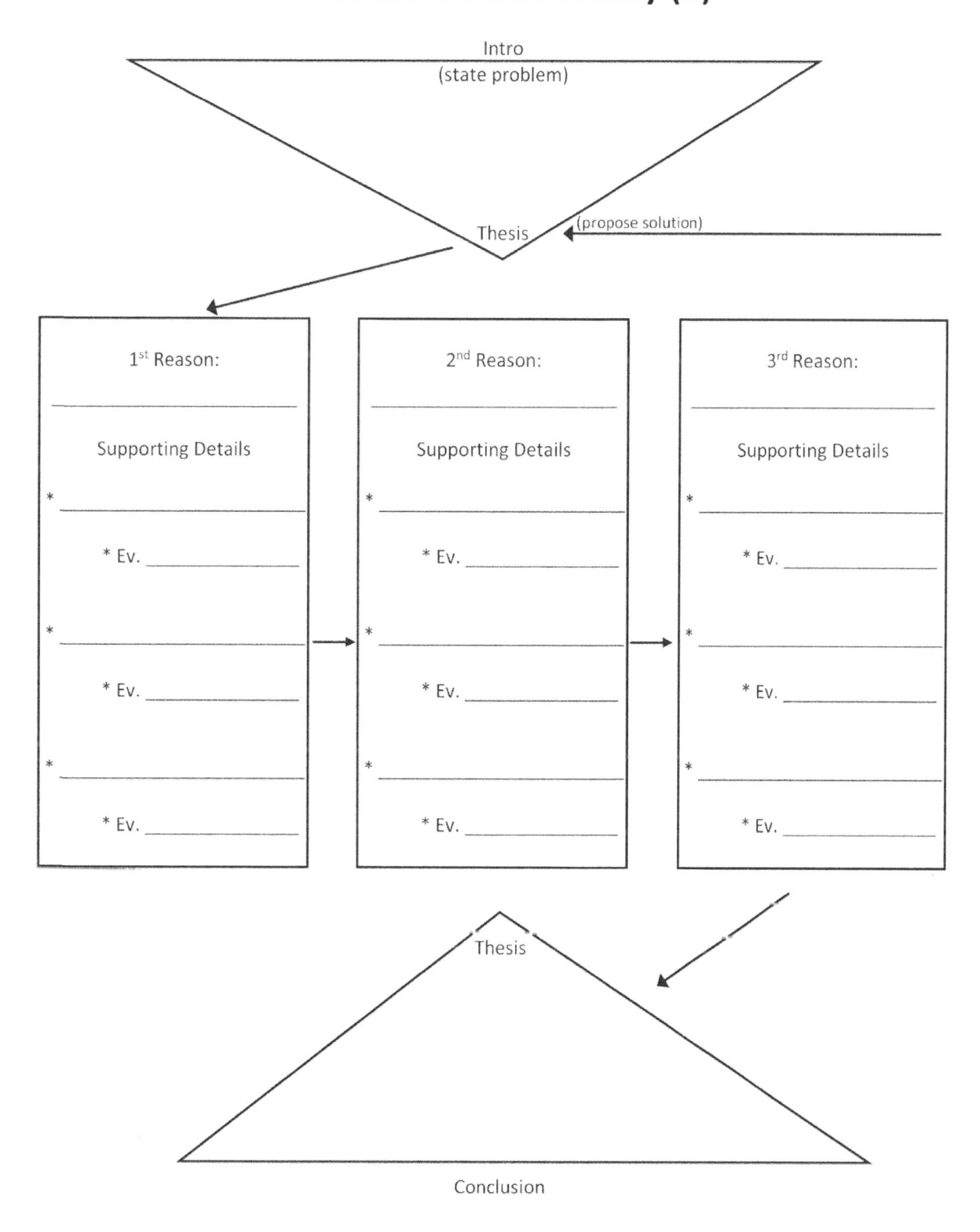

Intro
(state problem)

Thesis   (propose solution)

1st Reason: _____	2nd Reason: _____	3rd Reason: _____
Supporting Details	Supporting Details	Supporting Details
* _____	* _____	* _____
* Ev. _____	* Ev. _____	* Ev. _____
* _____	* _____	* _____
* Ev. _____	* Ev. _____	* Ev. _____
* _____	* _____	* _____
* Ev. _____	* Ev. _____	* Ev. _____

Thesis

Conclusion

©Powerhouse Educational Resources

Sample Introduction and Conclusion

Plastic Pollution Prevention

"More than 8 million tons of plastic are dumped in our oceans every year" ("The Facts"). We consume plastic at an incredible rate. Plastic is found in just about everything, and 50% of it is only used once. A huge amount of this waste is plastic bags. "Annually approximately 500 billion plastic bags are used worldwide. More than one million bags are used every minute" ("The Facts"). We can throw away everything. And, unfortunately, due to littering, wind, and rain washing it away, a lot of the plastic in our disposable world ends up in the ocean. As is easily apparent, the natural beauty of the oceans and coastlines suffers because of this. Animals easily mistake plastic for food and eagerly devour it, which leads to fatal choking and digestion problems. Additionally, they easily become fettered in loose pieces of plastic and drown or starve to death. From plastic bags to chewing gum, plastic of manifold shapes and sizes is flooding the oceans of the world (Lytle).

The first possible solution to this egregious quagmire is raising education and awareness...

A second solution to aid in reducing the waste in the ocean is to take personal responsibility...

A third remedy for this conundrum is governments and businesses taking responsibility...

In today's readily disposable world, plastic pollution is a huge problem. Literal tons of this waste ends up in the ocean. Unless sincere efforts are made to reduce the amount of plastic waste existing, the ocean will eventually become a wet garbage patch. Already, research is suggesting "that not one square mile of surface ocean anywhere on earth is free of plastic pollution" (Ocean Plastics Pollution). However, possible solutions to this enormous problem are evident. First, education and awareness need to be spread to the general public. Hopefully, this will lead to many individuals consciously deciding to take personal responsibility. Finally, businesses and governments around the world must initiate programs that will reduce and clean up plastic waste and also preserve wildlife habitats. If these solutions are put into place, the plastic pollution in our oceans will decrease and we will be headed toward a healthier and less garbage-filled world.

(Credit: Ivy A.)

In the paragraphs above, underline the thesis in the introduction and the conclusion.

Which graphic organizer was used? _____

Problem-Solution Essay Rubric

	Student	Teacher
Ideas		
Well-developed thesis	_____	_____
Clearly identifies problem (both organizers)	_____	_____
Proposes solution (organizer B)	_____	_____
Logical, realistic solution(s)	_____	_____
Depth of knowledge, insight	_____	_____
Thought-provoking	_____	_____
Organization		
Paragraphs		
Thesis	_____	_____
Body (3 clearly supportive paragraphs)	_____	_____
Conclusion (restates problem & summarizes solutions)	_____	_____
Appropriate transitions	_____	_____
Voice		
Demonstrates writer's interest in topic	_____	_____
Uses creative expressions, images	_____	_____
Word Choice		
Powerful verbs	_____	_____
Specific nouns	_____	_____
Rich vocabulary	_____	_____
Sentence Fluency		
Varied in size	_____	_____
Varied in structure	_____	_____
Conventions		
Appropriate punctuation	_____	_____
Correct grammar	_____	_____
Correct spelling	_____	_____
Presentation		
Typed in MLA format	_____	_____
Number of points		
Vocab words in essay (up to 5)	_____	_____
Total points/percentage	_____	_____

Colin Compton

Mrs. Dettinger

High School Composition

13 November 2013

A National Crisis

  Your average job doesn't involve much trauma. You might get stressed out when you spill your coffee or turn in a report a day late, but that's not trauma. However, certain professions experience it every day. One of these is the armed forces. The accumulated trauma accompanied with these jobs has led to a nationwide problem that few are willing to promulgate. That problem is military suicide. Day after day, these men and women are subject to intense stress. They don't know which civilian might open fire on them at any time. They don't know if the car up ahead has an active bomb in its trunk. They don't know if they'll ever be able to live normally again. Uncertainty is ubiquitous. It is things like these that weigh heavily on the minds of military personnel. Suicide often seems like the only way out of the emotional pain they experience. For every soldier killed in combat, 25 will commit suicide (Matt Wood). Clearly there is a nationwide epidemic that needs to be addressed. But what needs to be done? There are manifold steps that can be taken.

  One is counseling. Psychiatrists are essential to diagnosing Post Traumatic Stress Disorder and can offer proper treatment options. After soldiers have experience the nerve-racking strain of war, they often don't know how to re-adjust to civilian life or even just carry on with their service. Psychiatrists overseas and at home can help with this difficult process and talk them through the emotions they're dealing with. As a result, they must be easy to get in touch with and always be available to talk. Training and employing more military psychiatrists would be a simple way to reduce suicide rates.

Another step that could be taken is to shorten the length of tours for active duty soldiers. The military has started to do this by dropping the deployment length from 12 months to 9 months. However, most of the time shaved off has just been replaced with training exercises (Schindler). If a real difference is to be made, soldiers need to be able to spend time at home with their families. This allows them to unwind a bit and strengthen relationships that are put under stress because of long deployment. The amount of times a soldier is deployed could also be reduced. Some men serve four or five tours. That much time spent in combat wears on a soldier. If a two or three tour limit is placed on service, it would help reduce trauma levels.

Finally, a simple way to reduce military suicide is through support - not just a psychiatrist, but someone who is a close friend. Someone who is genuinely involved in their life and demonstrates that they care. We have Veterans Day and Memorial Day parades, but who is showing their appreciation the rest of the year? This solution isn't something that can be formatted like a program or organization. It requires individuals to step up and show their appreciation for veterans. They need to do this so that the daunting gap between combat and civilian life might be bridged. This story is a perfect example of the care veterans need. Army Sergeant Major Joseph Sanders attempted suicide twice. The first time he loaded a bullet in a revolver and pulled the trigger. But the metallic click of a cold empty chamber brought him to his senses. The second time he idled his car engine in a closed garage, but he realized how much he had to live for and knocked on a neighbor's door for help at 1:00 AM. His friend took him to a military chaplain that night, and he received the care he needed. Sanders said, "All it takes, you always have someone to turn to, someone that cares" (David Wood).

The egregious problem of military suicide is one that must be addressed by our nation. Our service men and women deserve support and care for the sacrifices they've made. They spend months away from their loved ones in hostile places so that others might enjoy the warmth of freedom. By giving them easy access to psychiatrists, shorter deployments, and support at home, we can reduce the suicide rates greatly. So, do you know a veteran you can reach out to today?

Works Cited

Meshad, Shad. "Some Thoughts on Suicide Prevention." *Huffington Post.com*. N.p., 12 Sep 2013. Web. 12 Nov 2013.

Schindler, Michael. "Shortened Deployment Cycles for 2012." *seattlepi.com*. Hearst Seattle Media, 24 Aug 2011. Web. 12 Nov 2013

Wood, David. "Military and Veteran Suicide Rise Despite Aggressive Prevention Efforts." *Huffington Post.com*. N.p., 29 Aug 2013. Web. 12 Nov 2013

Wood, Matt. "Crunching the Numbers of the Rate of Suicide Among Veterans." *SCIENCE LIFE.com*. N.p., 27 Apr 2012. Web. 12 Nov 2013.

Lesson 7
Argumentative Essays

Quiz #6

Matching

1. _____ transient
2. _____ quagmire
3. _____ zenith
4. _____ stupefy
5. _____ cogent
6. _____ promulgate
7. _____ tenuous
8. _____ ineffable
9. _____ ubiquitous
10. _____ cacophony
11. _____ malevolent
12. _____ veracity
13. _____ pugnacious
14. _____ neophyte
15. _____ fetter
16. _____ manifold
17. _____ iconoclast
18. _____ usurp
19. _____ serendipity

A. to seize by force or take possession without right
B. quarrelsome, combative
C. having little substance or strength
D. a difficult situation
E. intellectually convincing
F. someone who attacks common beliefs or institutions
G. diverse, varied
H. the highest point, the culminating point
I. luck; finding good things without looking for them
J. tremendous noise, disharmonious sound
K. wishing harm to others
L. a shackle or chain for the feet; a restraint
M. passing through briefly; passing into and out of existence
N. to proclaim or make known
O. truthfulness, accuracy
P. (seemingly) everywhere
Q. not able to express through words
R. someone who is young or inexperienced
S. to astonish, make insensible

Short Answer

If you were writing a Problem-Solution Essay about homelessness in your community, in what two ways could you organize it? Respond below.

20. One possible thesis (based on Graphic Organizer A):

21. Another possible thesis (based on Graphic Organizer B):

Lesson 7: The Argumentative Essay

Vocabulary for Lesson 7

Egregious:

Harangue:

Surmise:

Pulchritude:

___

The main difference between an argumentative essay and other essays is that in an argumentative essay, you must _____.

Considerations for the Argumentative Essay:

1. Decide if your position is the _____ or the _____ view.

2. Know the strongest arguments for _____ _____.

3. _____ why your view is superior.

4. Know the difference between a _____ conclusion and an _____ point of view.

5. _____ _____ is crucial, so be sure to _____ your _____.

Study the graphic organizers on the next two pages. Graphic Organizer B resembles another graphic organizer we've studied. Which one? _____

Essay of Argumentation (A)

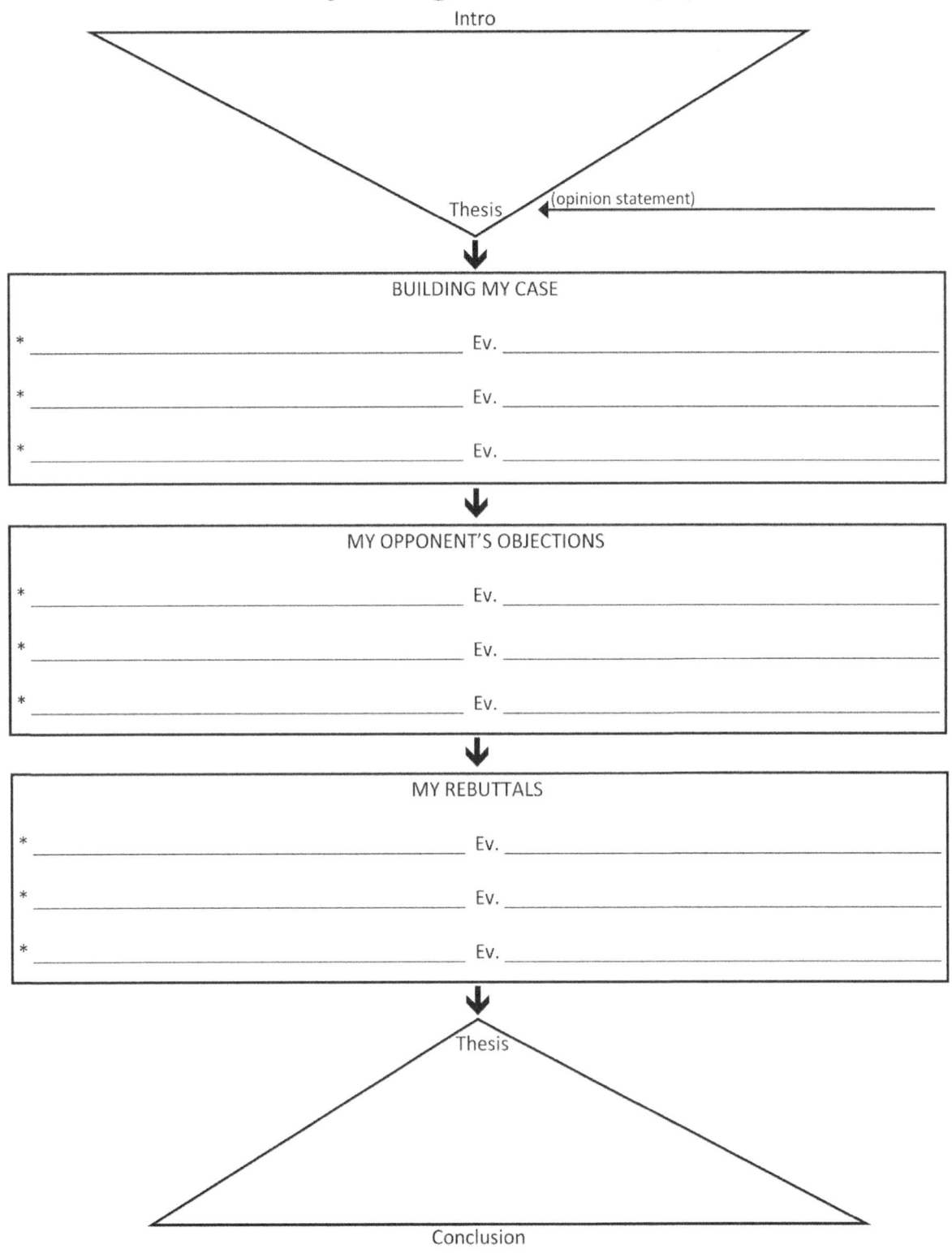

Intro

Thesis ← (opinion statement)

BUILDING MY CASE

* _____ Ev. _____
* _____ Ev. _____
* _____ Ev. _____

MY OPPONENT'S OBJECTIONS

* _____ Ev. _____
* _____ Ev. _____
* _____ Ev. _____

MY REBUTTALS

* _____ Ev. _____
* _____ Ev. _____
* _____ Ev. _____

Thesis

Conclusion

©Powerhouse Educational Resources

Essay of Argumentation (B)

Intro

Thesis ← (opinion statement)

OPPOSING VIEW: _____

Supporting Details/Evidence
- _____
- _____
- _____

1st Point: _____

MY REBUTTAL: _____

Supporting Details/Evidence
- _____
- _____
- _____

OPPOSING VIEW: _____

Supporting Details/Evidence
- _____
- _____
- _____

2nd Point: _____

MY REBUTTAL: _____

Supporting Details/Evidence
- _____
- _____
- _____

OPPOSING VIEW: _____

Supporting Details/Evidence
- _____
- _____
- _____

3rd Point: _____

MY REBUTTAL: _____

Supporting Details/Evidence
- _____
- _____
- _____

Thesis

Conclusion

©Powerhouse Educational Resources

The following is an article on MedlinePlus.Gov (from the U.S. National Library of Medicine). **Read it and decide if you are affirmative or negative.**
https://medlineplus.gov/ency/article/002432.htm

Genetically Engineered Foods

Genetically engineered (GE) foods have had their DNA changed using genes from other plants or animals. Scientists take the gene for a desired trait in one plant or animal, and they insert that gene into a cell of another plant or animal.

Function
Genetic engineering can be done with plants, animals, or bacteria and other very small organisms. Genetic engineering allows scientists to move desired genes from one plant or animal into another. Genes can also be moved from an animal to a plant or vice versa. Another name for this is genetically modified organisms, or GMOs.

The process to create GE foods is different than selective breeding. This involves selecting plants or animals with desired traits and breeding them. Over time, this results in offspring with those desired traits.

One of the problems with selective breeding is that it can also result in traits that are not desired. Genetic engineering allows scientists to select one specific gene to implant. This avoids introducing other genes with undesirable traits. Genetic engineering also helps speed up the process of creating new foods with desired traits.

The possible benefits of genetic engineering include:
- More nutritious food
- Tastier food
- Disease- and drought-resistant plants that require fewer environmental resources (such as water and fertilizer)
- Less use of pesticides
- Increased supply of food with reduced cost and longer shelf life
- Faster growing plants and animals
- Food with more desirable traits, such as potatoes that produce less of a cancer-causing substance when fried
- Medicinal foods that could be used as vaccines or other medicines

Some people have expressed concerns about GE foods, such as:
- Creating foods that can cause an allergic reaction or that are toxic
- Unexpected or harmful genetic changes
- Genes moving from one GM plant or animal to another plant or animal that is not genetically engineered
- Foods that are less nutritious

These concerns have proven to be unfounded. None of the GE foods used today have caused any of these problems. The US Food and Drug Administration (FDA) assesses all GE foods to make sure they are safe before allowing them to be sold. In addition to the FDA, the US Environmental Protection Agency (EPA) and the US Department of Agriculture (USDA) regulate bioengineered plants and animals. They assess the safety of GE foods to humans, animals, plants, and the environment.

Food Sources
Cotton, corn, and soybeans are the main GE crops grown in the United States. Most of these are used to make ingredients for other foods, such as:
- Corn syrup used as a sweetener in many foods and drinks
- Corn starch used in soups and sauces
- Soybean, corn, and canola oils used in snack foods, breads, salad dressings, and mayonnaise
- Sugar from sugar beets

Other major GE crops include:
- Apples
- Papayas
- Potatoes
- Squash

Side Effects
There are no side effects from consuming GE foods.

Recommendations
The World Health Organization, the National Academy of Science, and several other major science organizations across the globe have reviewed research on GE foods and found no evidence that they are harmful. There are no reports of illness, injury, or environmental harm due to GE foods. Genetically engineered foods are just as safe as conventional foods.
In the United States, labeling of genetically engineered foods is not required by the FDA. This is because there has been no significant difference found in nutrition or safety.

Alternative Names
Bioengineered foods; GMOs; Genetically modified foods

References
Hielscher S, Pies I, Valentinov V, Chatalova L. Rationalizing the GMO debate: the ordonomic approach to addressing agricultural myths. *Int J Environ Res Public Health*. 2016;13(5):476. PMID: 27171102. www.ncbi.nlm.nih.gov/pubmed/27171102.
National Academies of Sciences, Engineering, and Medicine. 2016. *Genetically Engineered Crops: Experiences and Prospects.* Washington, DC: The National Academies Press. doi: 10.17226/23395.
US Food and Drug Administration. Consumer info about food from genetically engineered plants. Updated October 19, 2015. www.fda.gov/food/ingredientspackaginglabeling/geplants/ucm461805.htm. Accessed July 14, 2016.
US Food and Drug Administration. How FDA regulates food from genetically engineered plants. Updated October 13, 2015. www.fda.gov/food/ingredientspackaginglabeling/geplants/ucm461831.htm. Accessed July 14, 2016.
US Food and Drug Administration. Questions & answers on food from genetically engineered plants. Updated November 23, 2015. www.fda.gov/food/ingredientspackaginglabeling/geplants/ucm346030.htm. Accessed July 14, 2016.
World Health Organization. Frequently asked questions on genetically modified foods. May 2014. www.who.int/foodsafety/areas_work/food-technology/Frequently_asked_questions_on_gm_foods.pdf. Accessed July 14, 2016.

Review Date 8/14/2016 Updated by: Emily Wax, RD, The Brooklyn Hospital Center, Brooklyn, NY. Also reviewed by David Zieve, MD, MHA, Isla Ogilvie, PhD, and the A.D.A.M. Editorial team.

After reading the article, is your view affirmative or negative? _____

Based on what you read in "Genetically Engineered Foods," write a thesis sentence for an argumentative essay in the *affirmative*.

_____
_____
_____

Based on what you read in "Genetically Engineered Foods," write a thesis sentence for an argumentative essay in the *negative*.

_____
_____
_____

A Values Debate

The following statement is a former resolution for the Lincoln-Douglas debate category for NCFCA, a national speech and debate organization.

Governments have a moral obligation to assist other nations in need.

After considering this statement, are you affirmative or negative? _____

List some reasons for your position:

"Governments have a moral obligation to assist other nations in need."

Affirmative	Negative	Rebuttal

"Governments do NOT have a moral obligation to assist other nations in need."

Negative	Affirmative	Rebuttal

Some Affirmative Evidence to Get You Started

"Governments **have** a moral obligation to assist other nations in need."

"Millions of lives have been saved through large-scale health interventions, many of them supported by aid programs. Routine immunizations save three million lives every year, smallpox was eradicated, polio has been nearly eradicated, an there has been enormous progress in fighting river blindness, guinea worm, diarrheal diseases, and others. Life expectancy has gone up around the world." Radelet, Steve, Ph.D. "The Effectiveness of Foreign Aid." Council on Foreign Relations. www.cfr.org/foreign-aid/effectiveness-foreign-aid/p12077. 01 December, 2006.

"Sure, lots of countries have done poorly. But several large aid recipients have done well, including Korea, Botswana, Taiwan, and more recently Mozambique, Ghana, and Tanzania. Egypt and Pakistan have tripled their incomes." Radelet, Steve, Ph.D. "The Effectiveness of Foreign Aid." Council on Foreign Relations. www.cfr.org/foreign-aid/effectiveness-foreign-aid/p12077. 01 December, 2006.

"The few studies that find no relationship between aid and growth are fragile, and rely on special and unrealistic assumptions, such as that each dollar of aid has the same impact with no diminishing returns, and that all aid is the same whether it is used to build roads or buy food for refugees."
Radelet, Steve, Ph.D. "The Effectiveness of Foreign Aid." Council on Foreign Relations. www.cfr.org/foreign-aid/effectiveness-foreign-aid/p12077. 01 December, 2006.

"When a disaster is of such a large scale, private organizations simply cannot administer aid on their own. In the case of Hurricane Katrina relief, despite the fact that so many domestic organizations gave aid, foreign nations and charities also offered substantial help, and the involvement of their governments was needed. For example, the United States formally asked the European Union to coordinate the aid offered by nations within the EU" ("Aftermath of Katrina Hurricane ").
"Aftermath of Katrina Hurricane: State of Play of EU Assistance to the US." The European Union Official Website. September 80, 2005. europa.eu/rapic/pressReleasesAction. Web.

There are a lot of misconceptions about the value of foreign aid, at times seen as some form of naïve humanitarianism. But modern foreign aid is not charity. It is strategic and an investment in a stronger America abroad. For example, South Korea was provided strategic foreign aid after the ceasefire on the Korean peninsula in 1953, creating one of

our most important allies and our 6th-largest trading partner. The return has been exponentially higher than the investment.
    "What's the real value of US foreign aid?" by Mina Chang, CNN.com, Updated 10:06 AM ET, Sat May 20, 2017.

The foreign aid budget in the U.S. for 2013 was just over one percent of the total federal budget.
    "2016 United States Budget Estimate." insidegov.com. 2014. Inside Gov. 4/1/2016. Web.

Some Negative Evidence to Get You Started

"Governments **do not have** a moral obligation to assist other nations in need."

Thomas Jefferson in his first inaugural address argued that the role of government was to pursue peace and friendships with all nations, but "entangling alliances with none."
    Thomas Jefferson First Inaugural Address, March 4, 1801. www.bartleby.com/124/pres16.html.

George Washington warned, in his farewell address, that "it is folly in one nation to look for disinterested favors from another; that it must pay with a portion of its independence for whatever it may accept under that character."
    Washington, George. "Farewell Address." yale.edu. 1796. Yale University. Web.

According to the U.S. Constitution, "Treason against the United States, shall consist only in levying War against them, or in adhering to their Enemies, giving them Aid or Comfort" (Article III, Section 3).

The estimated spending for (the U.S. in) 2016 was $3.59 trillion ("2016 United States Budget Estimate"), making the 1% foreign aid output "merely" $36 billion or so.
    "2016 United States Budget Estimate." insidegov.com. 2014. Inside Gov. 4/1/2016. Web.

"*Over the past 60 years at least $1 trillion of development-related aid has been transferred from rich countries to Africa. Yet real per-capita income today is lower than it* *was in the 1970s, and more than 50% of the population - over 350 million people - live on less than a dollar a day, a figure that has nearly doubled in two decades" (Moyo).*

    Moyo, Dambisa. The Wall Street Journal. "Why Foreign Aid is Hurting Africa." wsj.com. 21 March 2009. Dow Jones and Company. 02 November 2013. Web.

"Aid… has kept Africa behind, or Africans behind in terms of getting the confidence they need, the experience they need to take a full part in the global economy, create businesses that compete globally and succeed globally, because it has distorted markets in Africa" (Fal).

    Fal, Malik. "Malik Fal - Advocacy for Small-Medium Enterprises." *povertycure.org.* PovertyCure. 02 December 2013. Web.

"The definition of quality of life is in terms of the experience of individuals. If a person experiences her life as good and desirable, it is assumed to be so… factors such as feelings of joy, pleasure, contentment, and life satisfaction are paramount" (Diener, Suh).

    Diener, Ed; Suh, Eunkook. "Measuring Quality of Life: Economic, Social, and Subjective Indicators." forschungsnetzwerk.at. AMS Austria. Department of Labor Studies. 03 December 2013. Web.

Essay of Argumentation Rubric

	Student	Teacher
Ideas		
Focused thesis	_____	_____
Convincing arguments	_____	_____
Tactful presentation of opposing view	_____	_____
Holds reader's attention	_____	_____
Organization		
Paragraphs	_____	_____
Thesis clearly developed	_____	_____
Body	_____	_____
Case clearly developed	_____	_____
Writer's points well-supported	_____	_____
Conclusion summarizes and convicts	_____	_____
Appropriate transitions	_____	_____
Voice		
Demonstrates writer's interest in topic	_____	_____
Uses creative expressions, images	_____	_____
Word Choice		
Powerful verbs	_____	_____
Specific nouns	_____	_____
Rich vocabulary	_____	_____
Sentence Fluency		
Varied in size	_____	_____
Varied in structure	_____	_____
Conventions		
Appropriate punctuation	_____	_____
Correct grammar	_____	_____
Correct spelling	_____	_____
Presentation		
Typed in MLA format	_____	_____
Number of points		
Vocab words in essay (up to 5)	_____	_____
Total points/percentage	_____	_____

Kate Hancock

Mrs. Dettinger

High School Composition

25 March 2014

Government is Force

How can one rebuild after such egregious turmoil? This may have been the inquiry of many people as they witnessed the wreckage produced by the pugnaciously malevolent Typhoon Haiyan or Yolanda. A journalist Sarah Weaver inscribed this about the Philippines after the monster struck, "trees and power lines lie broken and mangled. Rubble is piled along the streets. And foundations or empty shells of homes stand as a reminder of the storm's strength." According to USAID, 6201 people were slaughtered, while 4.1 million were displaced. The citizens of the Philippines surely felt ineffably disheartened after such devastation. How could they begin anew? However, they did not stand alone. Several different organizations have been offering relief to the Philippines, such as USAID, the American Red Cross, the Salvation Army, and even Apple and Google according to nbcnews.com. Some of the organizations, such as USAID, are government agencies. Should foreign government be helping the Philippines? Do governments have a moral obligation to assist other nations in need? I believe not.

In order to grasp my point, it is wise to first understand what a few terms mean. What does "government" mean? According to the American Heritage dictionary "government" means "the office, function, or authority of a governing individual or body." Meanwhile, the definition of "assist" is "to give aid or support." Does "governing" match with "assisting?" My thesaurus thinks not. Looking at the word "moral," it is defined in *Webster's New Dictionary of the English*

Language as "relating to principles of right and wrong: conforming to a standard of right behavior." In this day and age can we associate "moral" with "government?" We can if a government is acting in accordance with laws based on virtuous moral principles. "The binding force of civility, kindness or gratitude, when the performance of a duty cannot be enforced by law" is the definition of "obligation" according to the 1828 Webster's Dictionary. Are governments satisfying needs out of the bottom of their hearts or do they have other motives? What does "need" mean? It is a seemingly insignificant word; however, it holds great weight. The Merriam Webster dictionary defines "need" as "a condition requiring supply or relief." What then is the proper role of government, to be a relief agency or a governing body? I believe it is out of bounds for a government to be a relief organization.

The opposite side believes that governments do have a moral obligation to assist other nations in need. Their reasons for this include that it makes the world a better place. Who wouldn't want that? In relation to a better world, the big rally cry is that government assistance ends poverty. In fact, the leading US government relief agency, USAID, declares their mission is to "...end extreme poverty and to promote resilient, democratic societies while advancing our security and prosperity." Another reason is world peace. For example, the 2012 joint report of the US State Department and USAID describes many ways that these government organizations can labor together with non-profit and international organizations to "help those affected by disaster to cope and then begin again by converting crisis situations into opportunities to promote peace, democracy, and economic growth" (22). Besides peace, many people justify governmental assistance through means of the veracities of the Bible, such as the article by Monte Asbury, entitled, "A Bible argument for government aid to the poor."

Even still, governments do not have a moral obligation to assist other nations in need. My point is simple. It is not the proper role of government. Before we can really debate whether or not governments have a moral obligation to assist other nations in need, it stands compulsory that we first understand governments' purpose, their proper role. Governments were not inaugurated to be stupefying charitable welfare programs. Grover Cleveland, a former president of the United States promulgated, "Though the people support government, the government should not support the people." The purpose of governments is not to pretend to be a pulchritudinous charity organization. Governments' purpose and limitations are explained quite well by Ezra Taft Benson, a former US Secretary of Agriculture (from 1953-1961) under former President Dwight D. Eisenhower, and H. Verlan Andersen in the book *The Proper Role of Government*. Andersen declares, "Governments are established primarily for the purpose of enforcing a code of moral behavior called criminal law" (23). Benson lists some things that the governments can do "by deriving its just powers from the governed, government becomes primarily a mechanism for defense against bodily harm, theft, and involuntary servitude" (6). The Declaration of Independence says that governments are called upon to protect the rights of the people.

> We hold these truths to be self-evident, that all men are created equal, that they Are endowed by their Creator with certain unalienable Rights, that among these are Life, Liberty and the pursuit of Happiness. -- That to secure these rights, Governments are instituted among Men, deriving their just powers from the consent of the governed...

The United States Constitution is ideal for all sound governments, for it was divinely given. While it is proper for a government to protect the rights of its people, it should not become a charity giver. Ezra Taft Benson has a solid opinion on this subject.

> But what about the needy? On the surface this may sound heartless and insensitive to the needs of those less fortunate individuals who are found in any society, no matter how affluent. "What about the lame, the sick, and the destitute?" is often the voiced question. Most other countries in the world have attempted to use the power of the government to meet this need. Yet, in every case, the improvement has been marginal at best and has resulted in the long run creating more misery, more poverty and certainly less freedom than when the government first stepped in. (15)

Author Henry D. Thoreau would surely agree with the above statement, for he made one quite similar.

> This government never of itself furthered any enterprise, but by the alacrity with which it got out of its way. It does not keep the country free. It does not settle the West. It does not educate. The character inherent in the American people has done all that has been accomplished; and it would have done somewhat more, if the government had not sometimes go in its way. (Thoreau)

Remember that the end does not justify the means, not matter now innocent the end.

My clear concise reason that I do not believe that governments have a moral obligation to assist other nations in need is that it is simply not the proper role of government. Once we understand governments' role, I believe that all other issues such as this will be quickly resolved. Because America's government was divinely created and remained in its proper place, we have thus prospered. However, we have strayed far from our roots, which straying will eventually lead to our demise. Look at the nations all around that are struggling in quagmires. "All we like sheep have gone astray; we have turned everyone to his own way..." (Isaiah 53:4). It's time to cease straying and reign in our governments, fettering it back down in its proper place. As George Washington once decreed, "Government is not reason; it is not eloquent; it is force."

Works Cited

Asbury, Monte. "A Bible argument for government aid to the poor." masbury.wordpress.com WordPress.com. 22 March 2014.

"Assist." ahdictionary.com. 2014. Houghton Mifflin Harcourt. 21 March 2014

Benson, Ezra Taft and H. Verlan Andersen. *The Proper Role of Government*. USA: Archive Publishers. 1995. Print.

"Civil Disobedience- Part 1 or 3." thoreau.eserver.org. 21 March 2014.

"George Washington Quotes." brainyquote.com. 2014. BookRags Media Network. 21 March 2014.

"Government." ahdictionary.com. 2014. Houghton Mifflin Harcourt. 21 March 2014.

"Grover Cleveland Quotes." brainyquote.com. 2014. BookRags Media Network. 21 March 2014.

"How to help: Organizations offering relief to Typhoon Haiyan survivors." nbcnews.com 21 March 2014.

"Joint Summary of Performance and Financial Information for FY 2012." state.gov. US State Department. 22 March 2014

"Mission, Vision and Values." usaid.gov. 2014. 21 March 2014.

"Need." merriam-webster.com. 2014. Merriam-Webster, Incorporated. 21 March 2014

"Obligation." 1828.mshaffer.com. 2014. 21 March 2014.

"Philippines - Typhoon Yolanda/Haiyan." usaid.gov. 2014. 21 March 2014.

"The Declaration of Independence: A Transcription." archives.gov. 21 March 2014.

Weaver, Sarah Jane. "Philippines Recovering One Nail at a Time." lds.org. 2014. Intellectual Reserve, Inc. 21 March 2014.

Webster's New Dictionary of the English Language. Federal Street Press, 2002. Print.

Lesson 8
Test Prep

Quiz # 7

Matching

1. _____ egregious
2. _____ transient
3. _____ usurp
4. _____ quagmire
5. _____ iconoclast
6. _____ zenith
7. _____ manifold
8. _____ stupefy
9. _____ fetter
10. _____ cogent
11. _____ neophyte
12. _____ harangue
13. _____ promulgate
14. _____ surmise
15. _____ pugnacious
16. _____ tenuous
17. _____ serendipity
18. _____ pulchritude
19. _____ ineffable
20. _____ malevolent
21. _____ ubiquitous
22. _____ cacophony
23. _____ veracity

A. someone who is young or inexperienced
B. not able to express through words
C. extremely bad
D. to infer with little evidence
E. the highest point, the culminating point
F. to proclaim or make known
G. to seize by force or take possession without right
H. to astonish, make insensible
I. tremendous noise, disharmonious sound
J. a shackle or chain for the feet; a restraint
K. diverse, varied
L. a ranting speech
M. someone who attacks common beliefs or institutions
N. wishing harm to others
O. intellectually convincing
P. (seemingly) everywhere
Q. a difficult situation
R. quarrelsome, combative
S. physical beauty
T. having little substance or strength
U. truthfulness, accuracy
V. luck; finding good things without looking for them
W. passing through briefly; passing into and out of existence

Short Answer

24. What is the main difference between an argumentative essay and other types of persuasive essays?

_____
_____

True or False

25. _____ You rarely need to document evidence for an argumentative essay.

26. _____ An argumentative essay should reach a logical conclusion.

27. _____ If you create evidence for an argumentative essay, be sure it's emotional enough to convince the reader.

Lesson 8: Test Preparation

Remember the following when writing ANY essays:

1) 3 essential components
    a) _____
    b) _____
    c) _____
2) Vary sentence structure and _____.
3) Use _____ words.
4) Write _____.
    a) Get to the point.
    b) Avoid redundant words and concepts.
    c) Avoid "common knowledge."
5) Use _____ voice (subject of sentence = performer of action).
6) Be _____ in your evidence. Use proper nouns when appropriate.
7) Employ _____ words.

Strategies for timed essay test (particularly ACT):

1) Take a _____. (Don't be wishy-washy.)
    a) Use the one that's _____ to support.
    b) (Often has 2 other opposing views presented.)
2) Understand the format: 3 analytical jobs
    a) Express _____.
    b) Evaluate other _____.
    c) Discuss _____ between the three.
3) Outline
    a) Picture Graphic Organizer _____ to organize.

b) Break info down into simplest pieces (bottom lines).
   i) Your position in one phrase.
   ii) Other position in one phrase.
   iii) Other position in one phrase.

4) Budget your _____. (Bring your _____.)
   a) Pre-writing/planning: _____ minutes.
   b) Writing: _____ minutes (for ACT).
      i) The SAT writing test is 50 minutes total, so use 40 minutes to write for that.
   c) Proof-reading/editing: _____ minutes.

5) More writing helps
   a) Write _____, but do not skip lines.
   b) If your 3rd body paragraph isn't working:
   c) Support ideas with _____!
      i) _____ examples (applicable relevant situation).
      ii) _____ examples ("Suppose Johnny…")
      iii) _____ of vague or subjective terms.
      iv) _____ ("In my experience, 50% of high schoolers…").
      v) Memorized _____ (especially for intros and conclusions).
   d) Practice.

** The next two pages contain a sample writing prompt.**

First, read through all three steps below, then follow the directions.

1) Set a timer for 5 minutes.

2) Read the prompt on the next **two** pages.

3) Within the allotted time, create a basic outline for your essay on the practice page following the prompt.

   a) Visualize the graphic organizer as you create your prompt.

   b) Stop at 5 minutes.

Technology in the Classroom

Technology is an essential tool in our modern world, so it is not surprising that its use has become ubiquitous in K-12 classrooms as well. According to recent polls, seven in ten teachers claim that having state-of-the-art IT (information technology) equipment is more important than investing in traditional textbooks. However, some people feel there are significant downsides to students having "screen time" throughout their school day, citing studies that students comprehend more and respond better to textbook-based lessons. Given the increasing prevalence of this educational trend, it is worth examining the implications of digital textbooks replacing traditional textbooks in classrooms.

Read and carefully consider these perspectives. Each suggests a particular way of thinking about the increasing the use of technology and decreasing use of textbooks in K-12 classrooms.

Perspective One	Perspective Two	Perspective Three
Replacing textbooks with expensive technology in K-12 classrooms is inefficient. The financial demands of purchasing and maintaining new technology can be burdensome, particularly for economically disadvantaged school districts.	The students of today will be the leaders of tomorrow. In order to meet the demands of an increasingly technological global society, schools need to implement the tools their students will need to succeed and lead the next generation.	K-12 textbooks provide a fundamental learning medium that should not be uprooted by digital media's fast-paced entertainment. Replacing books with technology creates a generation that is more easily distracted and has increasingly shorter attention spans.

Essay Task
Write a unified, coherent essay about textbooks being replaced by technology in K-12 schools. In your essay, be sure to:

• clearly state your own perspective on the issue and analyze the relationship between your perspective and at least one other perspective

• develop and support your ideas with reasoning and examples

• organize your ideas clearly and logically

• communicate your ideas effectively in standard written English. Your perspective may be in full agreement with any of those given, in partial agreement, or completely different.

Planning Your Essay
Your work on these prewriting pages will not be scored. You may wish to consider the following as you think critically about the task:

Strengths and weaknesses of different perspectives on the issue
    • What insights do they offer, and what do they fail to consider?
    • Why might they be persuasive to others, or why might they fail to persuade?

Your own knowledge, experience, and values
    • What is your perspective on this issue, and what are its strengths and weaknesses?
    • How will you support your perspective in your essay?

Outline Practice Page

After your five-minute practice...

1. Speak your essay out loud based on your outline. This should take at least five minutes.
2. Repeat the process of speaking it out loud. Elaborate more on your supporting evidence this time. Aim for about six to eight minutes of speaking time.
3. Once you've spoken your essay a couple times, set your timer for 30 minutes to write and edit your essay on lined paper.

After completing the steps above, use another sample essay prompt to practice a timed essay from start to finish.

For more practice writing an ACT timed essay test, go to act.org.

For practice writing the SAT timed essay test, go to collegereadiness.collegeboard.org/sample-questions/essay.

*You may choose to use the rubric on the following page for evaluating your practice essay.

Practice Timed Essay Rubric

	Student	Teacher	Comments

Ideas
Clear Thesis   _____ _____
Supportive examples   _____ _____
Depth of knowledge, insight   _____ _____
Holds reader's attention   _____ _____
Well-crafted conclusion   _____ _____

Organization
Paragraphs
   Thesis (attention-getter, tie-in, thesis)   _____ _____
   Body (at least 2 supportive paragraphs)   _____ _____
   Conclusion (summarizes thesis)   _____ _____
Appropriate transitions   _____ _____

Voice
Uses creative expressions, images   _____ _____

Word Choice
Powerful verbs   _____ _____
Specific nouns   _____ _____
Rich vocabulary   _____ _____

Sentence Fluency
Varied in size   _____ _____
Varied in structure   _____ _____

Conventions
Appropriate punctuation   _____ _____
Correct grammar   _____ _____
Correct spelling   _____ _____

Presentation
Neatly formatted   _____ _____
Legible   _____ _____

Points out of 80   _____ _____
Extra Credit Vocabulary Earned (up to 5 pts) _____ _____
Total Percentage for Essay Portion   _____ _____

Final Test

Your final test is available at PowerHouseEdu.com or on your USB flash drive.

The first half looks like a larger version of your quizzes.

The second half is the timed essay. For this, be sure to have lined paper ready for your prewriting (outline) as well as your written essay. Also, ask someone else to print it for you (or to have it ready on your screen) so you do not see the prompt until your 40-minute timer has started.

Final Timed Essay Rubric

	Rank	Comments
Ideas		
Clear Thesis	_____	
Supportive examples	_____	
Depth of knowledge, insight	_____	
Holds reader's attention	_____	
Well-crafted conclusion	_____	
Organization		
Paragraphs		
Thesis (attention-getter, tie-in, thesis)	_____	
Body (at least 2 supportive paragraphs)	_____	
Conclusion (summarizes thesis)	_____	
Appropriate transitions	_____	
Voice		
Uses creative expressions, images	_____	
Word Choice		
Powerful verbs	_____	
Specific nouns	_____	
Rich vocabulary	_____	
Sentence Fluency		
Varied in size	_____	
Varied in structure	_____	
Conventions		
Appropriate punctuation	_____	
Correct grammar	_____	
Correct spelling	_____	
Presentation		
Neatly formatted	_____	
Legible	_____	

Points out of 80 _____

Extra Credit Vocabulary Earned (up to 5 pts) _____

Total Percentage for Essay Portion _____

Answer Keys

Answer Key: Quizzes

Quiz #1 (page 16)
1. B
2. D
3. A
4. C
5. Organization, depth of knowledge/insight, vocabulary/language
6. (Any of these three) Add more powerful parts of speech, use an appositive, play with syntax, add a clause, use a gerund.
7. Expository = informs; objective. Persuasive = informs AND persuades the reader to think or to act on an issue.
8. False
9. True
10. True
11. False
12. False

Quiz #2 (page 30)
1. C
2. F
3. A
4. G
5. H
6. B
7. D
8. E
9. Decide thesis (and/or choose your graphic organizer).
10. See graphic organizer on page 14.
11. False
12. True
13. True

Quiz #3 (page 44)
1. I
2. H
3. G
4. B
5. D
6. K
7. C

8. J
9. E
10. F
11. A
12. One cause with three effects or on effect with three causes
13. (Answers will vary. An opening sentence is meant to get the reader's attention.) Example: Over 600,000 Americans died in the Civil War.
14. (Answers will vary. A thesis statement will summarize the main idea of the essay.) Cause-effect thesis example: Three events contributed to our nation's Civil War.
15. (Answers will vary. A conclusion for a cause-effect essay usually ends with what ultimately happened.) Example: Ultimately, the bells of freedom will continue to ring in our country for centuries to come.

Quiz #4 (page 56)
1. J
2. H
3. G
4. F
5. A
6. E
7. C
8. L
9. K
10. M
11. N
12. D
13. I
14. B
15. Expository
16. Compare-contrast essay
17. Cause-effect essay
18. Persuasive
19. Process
20. See graphic organizers on pages 46-47. The Block Method may be either one block of similarities and one block of differences OR one block of "x" and one block of "y."

Quiz #5 (page 74)
1. K
2. G

3. E
4. H
5. O
6. L
7. M
8. D
9. A
10. C
11. B
12. I
13. P
14. J
15. N
16. F
17. Persuasive
18. (Answers will vary.) Example: We need a community pool.
19. ◊ Diamond-shaped
20. The point at the bottom of the diamond represents a specific call to action or belief for the reader.

Quiz #6 (page 86)
1. M
2. D
3. H
4. S
5. E
6. N
7. C
8. Q
9. P
10. J
11. K
12. O
13. B
14. R
15. L
16. G
17. F
18. A
19. I

20. (Answers will vary. This thesis should identify the problem and propose that there are three potential solutions.) Example: Homelessness is a problem in our community, and there are three ways we can unite to solve it.
21. (Answers will vary. This thesis will identify the problem and propose a solution.) Example: By equipping the homeless with tools to create income, we can solve this egregious problem.

Quiz #7 (page 108)
1. C
2. W
3. G
4. Q
5. M
6. E
7. K
8. H
9. J
10. O
11. A
12. L
13. F
14. D
15. R
16. T
17. V
18. S
19. B
20. N
21. P
22. I
23. U
24. An argumentative essay requires the writer to present *both* sides well.
25. False
26. True
27. False

Answer Key for final test is available at PowerHouseEdu.com or on your USB flash drive.

Made in the USA
Monee, IL
25 August 2023